Dr. Michael Palmieri is an American investor, pharmacist, and author. For the past decade, he has served as a pharmacy supervisor and laboratory director for a Fortune 100 retail chain. He holds a Bachelor of Science in biology and psychology, as well as a Doctorate of Pharmacy from the Massachusetts College of Pharmacy and Health Sciences University in Boston, Massachusetts. Palmieri has extensive experience investing in equity markets, and constructed a seven-figure portfolio by his early 30s. He has helped countless people transform their lives and personal finances. He is passionate about his family, being a patient advocate to improve health outcomes, fitness, and helping others build generational wealth. He is married to Annie Palmieri; they currently have two children.

This book is dedicated to my wife, Annie, and sons, Kaidan and Kilian. The motivation and inspiration you provide is the most powerful force I'll ever know.

Michael Palmieri

QUIET MIKE SPEAKS

THE NEW AGE GUIDE TO GENERATIONAL WEALTH

AUSTIN MACAULEY PUBLISHERS™

LONDON • CAMBRIDGE • NEW YORK • SHARJAH

Ordering Information
Quantity sales: Special discounts are available on quantity purchases by corporations, associations, and others. For details, contact the publisher at the address below.

Publisher's Cataloging-in-Publication data
Palmieri, Michael
Quiet Mike Speaks

ISBN 9781647506896 (Paperback)
ISBN 9781647506902 (ePub e-book)

Library of Congress Control Number: 2021912949

www.austinmacauley.com/us

First Published (2021)
Austin Macauley Publishers LLC
40 Wall Street, 33rd Floor, Suite 3302
New York, NY 10005
USA

mail-usa@austinmacauley.com
+1 (646) 5125767

To Annie, without your support, adding this valuable source of wealth to many, would not be possible.

To my sons, Kaidan and Kilian, who changed how I see the world.

To my editors and the Austin Macauley team, for believing in the work and manicuring it into the masterpiece it is today.

Disclosure Statement

The text ahead contains characters whose names and characteristics have been changed.

Although this book is designed to add value and aims to be accurate regarding the subject matter, it is listed for sale with the understanding that investing, and all investments involve risk. Neither the author or publisher is offering personalized investing or financial advice regarding any specific portfolio, investing style, security, or financial decision. The content should not be confused as financial advice, or a replacement for professional services in the areas of finance, legal, investment, accounting, tax, or any other thinkable or related monetary services. Readers should consider consulting a competent professional in the areas of financial planning and advising prior to making financial decisions. The text within is not a replacement any other financial services. Past performance does not guarantee future results, and investing can result in substantial financial losses.

Regarding the content discussed, to our knowledge it represents accurate data, but no warranty is made with respect to any claims, completeness, or accuracy of any information presented. Regulations, laws, and tax code are subject to change which may render certain passages irrelevant or inaccurate. It is the responsibility of the reader

to seek trusted and competent sourc
decisions.

The text is not intended to justify an
and the reader should understand that m
possibility that should be wagered at th
advised that readers clearly read and
prospectus of any potential investment they
and make their own informed judgment, befo
monetary commitments, regarding any thinkab
investment vehicle. Any specific securities, e
investment vehicles that are mentioned are
illustration purposes only and are not recomme
There is no warranty offered with respect to any info
contained within.

The author and publisher specifically deny and disc
any responsibility for any thinkable losses, damages, or
incurred indirectly or directly as a consequence of a
thinkable utility of the contents within this book
Investment vehicles are not FDIC insured nor bank
guaranteed and may lose value.

You are encouraged to consult your tax or legal advisors before making any financial decisions.

Preface

The typical life of an American worker is like Groundhog Day. Wake up early, and work hard five of seven days per week. For most, all they have to show for their efforts is debt, tax collections, and making their corporation richer.

We are trained from early on to become part of this broken record. Whether realized or not, we all work for the government, banks, and corporations; eager to become a taxable citizen and accumulating liabilities along the way.

Michael Palmieri identified this early. He followed the advice of his parents to study hard, earn a degree, and find a stable job. But quickly realized he was trapped in the "clock puncher" hustle. There was plenty of wealth to be obtained, but where did it come from? He studied feverishly to determine how the wealth gap emerges. The most approachable answer was investing.

From then on, his mindset changed. Walking around in public, he'd study people and behaviors to determine the latest consumer trends, monitoring checkout lines at physical stores and user traffic on consumer websites, and paying closer attention to the advertising on boards at the Stanley Cup than the players getting checked into them.

What transpired was a seven-figure net worth in his early 30s and this guide to add value to anyone who seeks it. A wake-up call to "the herd" to help build generational wealth.

As a man eager to assist others before himself, the most valuable contribution he could make was this book. The content within is what Wall Street doesn't want you to know. It needed to be written. Utilizing the strategies ahead and a little experience, it's probable you'll build a sizable portfolio and break the habits that guarantee most fall short of financial freedom.

These are exciting times to invest that require more than the average amount of knowledge. The wisdom within this book is what's needed to navigate today's markets in acquiring and retaining wealth. Like the Australian Wombat, it's soft and cute at first glance, but will forage and dig to reveal strategies and methods needed to achieve financial freedom.

Prologue

My friends and family were always envious of my financial position and asked me what book to read. The answer was there wasn't one book. The list would contain hundreds. I wanted to simplify. They all had been too busy living the "American dream."

I'd often ask, "When are you going to start investing?"

Their responses were alarmingly similar, "In a few years when the kids are grown," or, "My house is my investment, going to work on paying that off."

They were making a multi-million-dollar mistake.

I was flooded with questions at get-togethers, "How much do I need to invest to get rich?" and, "What stock should I buy?"

Most people have heard about investing, but the term can be frightening. What if I lose all my money? The financial institutions and press want you to think investing is difficult. Their jobs depend on it. This book will discuss how becoming financially free is a choice anyone can make.

Taking the road less traveled is what separates the middle class from the uber wealthy. If you are willing to do what's necessary and have a bit of common sense, keep reading. We'll compare the paths of a saver, spender, and an investor to demonstrate the magnitude of wealth those living the American dream are giving up.

Like a pilot, it's essential to plan for unexpected turbulence and pack a little extra gas (or plan your route past some battery chargers). Either way, buckle up and enjoy the journey to wealth.

The Wealthy Truth

Who's wealthy and how can we define "being rich."

Is it how many cars are lined up in the driveway? How many square feet your home is? How big your salary is? Most people looking to get rich follow the educational path. They search the web for top paying careers, and their screen fills with doctors, dentists, engineers, etc.

The keyword is "career." Google dictionary defines a career as "an occupation undertaken for a *significant period of a person's life* with opportunities for progress."

They are searching for the wrong information. Being rich and wealthy are two different things. Rich can be described as having purchasing power that exceeds the average person. Wealth is the ability to cover expenses without working.

Adjust your search to the wealthiest individuals in the United States, you will find a list that contains investors, business owners, or their heirs.

Can you enjoy life with much less and working paycheck to paycheck? Absolutely! But that's another book.

This one is about how to build generational wealth so your grandchildren's grandchildren can pursue their passions without worry. If you're intrigued by that, keep reading.

Unclaimed Property

Ever wonder who owns those beautiful homes in the next town? The perfectly manicured lawn and castle-like gated entries. The hedges were neatly hedged. The owners have one thing in common; nobody's home. Most are working overtime to keep the lights on.

There's a common denominator amongst people I know with big salaries. No matter how much they made, they were still working. They had some toys but were not rich. They always talked about how it wasn't enough. The more money earned, the more they burned.They had little time outside work, getting lost in the thick of thin things.

Salary is only a tool. If you don't understand its utility, it doesn't matter how much you make. Did anyone else just get an image of "the rock" in their head? Sure, salary can greatly improve your wealth potential. But it can equally be your adversary.

Do you know someone with a "high salary?" So do they (And so does the person they know)! Guess what. It's likely not enough for them either. They're still working through 65 and beyond, or until they can't. There's another way that is rarely taught. We'll cover it in detail.

People question why I don't label salary is a major determinant of wealth. For most, every $100 earned translates to around $60 after deductions. Before I was married several years ago I had reasonable savings and investment accounts, and a surplus of people egging me on to "start my life." "Buy a house" they said. "Sell your stocks and settle down." "Start a family." I could have easily listened to common rhetoric. If I did, things would we QUITE different today. But I skipped the first two.

Most focus on obtaining their lifestyle of choice first with their earnings, then consider investing what's "left over." I did the opposite. I pursued several opportunities; one of which was an investment in Tesla. Today, each $100 invested is worth over $2,500. Pay attention to who you are listening to. If you focus on your goals first, then settle down, the sacrifice will serve your wallet kindly.

Want to judge true wealth? Here's a method that doesn't discriminate amongst income classes with no formulas required. If you stopped working today, how long could you "keep the lights on?" If your answer is "not very long," or you are laughing, read on.

Some of my colleagues worked up the ranks to "senior" leadership, presidents, or CEO's. Several even earning salaries beyond $1,000,000 annually. I always looked up to them. But through conversations, I could see salary wasn't enough. And the only thing these "senior" executives had in common was, they were working until they were "senior" citizens. They always needed more money and talked about people they knew that were "really rich." They lived paycheck to paycheck on a grandiose scale with more payments and much bigger ones.

The problem with money is it's easy to spend. And there's no limit. Have a big salary? There's a consumer line of services and materials right in your wheelhouse! And banks are on deck to finance against future earnings. It's a challenge to escape clever day to day marketing for non-essential goods. Even if you stick to the basics; shelter, transportation, food, and healthcare, you can easily dig a deep hole.

At the time of this writing, the average home price in the US hovers around $230,000 while the average take-home pay is $38,000 after taxes. It's a challenge to comprehend; the price of basic shelter will cost most families 30 years of spending half of their salary on a mortgage. The price of some essentials has become so inflated they are out of reach to the majority without financing. I'd argue, we are more economically disadvantaged than most times in history. But it doesn't seem that way for one simple reason: loans. We can afford the monthly payment, but not the actual product. If you plan your finances based on your monthly allotment, you will spend what you earn monthly, yearly, and lifely? Did we just create a new word? Imagine how your life would change without loans. Although they can have some adverse effects, loans can play a major role in building wealth, if you play your cards right.

How many people do you know that paid cash for their home? Their car? Their kitchen table? Like me, probably none. Financing your life has become the norm to the point we don't question. We'll discuss how you can break the cycle.

The Fragile Fantasy

"If you wanna get out of the hole, first you gotta put down the shovel."

Rick Dicker – Incredibles 2

There are three key reasons lay people fail to build wealth: 1) their top three expenses, 2) they don't invest, and 3) they can't manage money. We will attack all three head on.

Growing up, my parents never told me about investing. They talked about "saving for a rainy day." I wondered, if they know so much about saving, why are they still working into their 50s and 60s?? Shouldn't those be the "golden years?" To a 16-year-old, their salaries seemed gigantic. How could they possibly spend all that money? The average household [1]income in 2018 was around $75,000, while the average annual expenditures were $67,500 (and rise in kind proportion with income). They were not alone.[2]Worse,

---

[1] https://www.fool.com/retirement/2018/04/29/how-does-the-average-american-spend-their-paycheck.aspx

[2] https://www.financialsamurai.com/what-percent-of-americans-own-stocks/

barely 50% of people invest a penny. And those who do; mutual funds (we'll discuss later) The moral? DON'T listen to your parents (at least when it comes to money).

For most, the more we earn, the more we spend. Why work hard and not enjoy your "success?" The answer is to build wealth. It can be a challenge to be frugal when big earnings start pouring in.

I found this challenging early in my career. Working hard for nine years to earn two degrees, one being a doctorate. At the age of 26, I felt I deserved it. Excited to impress my "clan" after graduation, I fled to the Audi dealer to pick up my custom ordered race red S4. Disappointingly, the first order was totaled. But thankfully, not by me. The car was flooded at the warehouse during a heavy rainstorm. Don't worry. They built me another one. I thought about getting that car for years. I was a success! Until the payments started coming in.

Riddled with $225,000 in student debt, a luxury apartment, and a new sports car, I got locked in a lifestyle that consumed my income and was damaging my financial future. I was taught it was normal, leveraging my expectation of future earnings to finance "stuff" I didn't need. I even bought a pickup truck to spare the Audi of grueling New England winters. Unfortunately, Facebook likes couldn't pay the bills (at least in this instance). I created a fragile fantasy that could have collapsed at any moment. Stuck on the wrong side of the assets vs. liabilities equation, it got me nowhere fast. I needed to make a change.

My cousins heart attack was the first hint I was heading down the wrong path. I vividly remember the day I got the call. How could it be, someone that had things so together and was healthy on the surface? He was a model of perfection; senior title, fancy cars, big house, and lifestyle I thought I wanted.

However, big titles and financial responsibilities come with big stress. This can be the culprit of many serious health problems, such as anxiety, depression, and cardiovascular disease. He hid it well, but the stress was brewing negative effects on his body. After several hours of surgery and multiple stents, he was back at the grind.

Two years later, I could see the angst in his eyes, chatting about his brother's new ride. Juggling payments for three Porsche's, two Mercedes, one Ferrari (and a partridge in a pear tree), among others. He quickly pointed to the desire to have something better.

Early in my career, I took things too seriously. I had a constant urgency to climb the ladder of success. I remember stressing when some bigwig was scheduled to visit our work site. Working myself up, they'd fly the company jet in, leave notes to vacuum beneath the counter, and fly back out to Timbuktu. It wasn't worth the hype.

There will always be someone who has climbed the career success ladder higher and has the next best thing.

But let's be honest. Being broke sucks. I recently misplaced a $20 bill. Owning a Michael Kors jacket, the pockets are shallow and set in an awkward position. It could have been hung on the wrong side of the store. I never carry cash, but that day had a $20 and a $1 bill. I hate storing anything in my pockets to begin with and have a notorious history for misplacing anything important. Of course, I lost $20. Don't worry, the $1 bill was safe and sound. But it didn't feel good. Whether you are happy or sad, wealth status exemplifies your feelings.

It temporarily feels good to reward yourself. But if you build wealth first, you'll permanently thank yourself later. Few people at age 45 would wish they had a nicer car when they were 20. If given the choice between wealth and better materials in the past, they'll take the cash and run. Waving "bye, Felicia" to work and the time clock.

But were getting a bit off track. How does this relate to building wealth? It's not necessarily the size of your income that builds wealth; it's if, when, and how you put money to work. It's also about living within your means.

Consistently setting aside a portion of your income; at least five percent is a good start. The more you can afford, the better. Focus on living on a portion of your income that's feasible, say 70%, and invest the remainder directly from your paycheck.

Take a hard look at your personal situation. Are you chasing the illusion for desire, or would you rather build wealth? The earlier the better. As you age, desires get more expensive. It can be hard to go "backward" in lifestyle. But if you're living beyond your means and building wealth is your goal, it may be essential. If you buy into Joneses rivalries before building wealth, you'll accumulate an average Joe net worth. Many people of purpose prefer to lock in their fair share. We'll discuss how.

To Buy Or Not to Buy, That is the Question

In the movie 'Meet the Parents', Pam's ex-fiancé, Kevin, was a stock trader. One of the most memorable scenes is when Pam's family holds her sister's engagement party at Kevin's mansion. The one with the Bolivian wormwood floors.

He asks Greg in the kitchen, "Are you a homeowner, Greg?"

Embarrassingly, he replies, "No, no, I rent."

Pam gives Greg a reassuring gesture, realizing it's frowned upon at their age not to own a home. That's exactly how we are made to feel nowadays, being elder and peer-pressured into a financial obligation we can't really afford.

They moved on to discussing finances, where Kevin asks Greg, "How's your portfolio?"

Greg replies, "Strong...to quite strong."

Like most people, we can gather from his tone, Greg has no portfolio.

A common mantra of elders regarding homeownership is, "You have to live somewhere!"

In our society, we're not considered to be independent or successful without carrying a boatload of loans. Don't worry about that big number! You'll pay it off before you're six feet under. But is home ownership really the investment it's cracked up to be? Some people may agree to disagree with my answer.

A close couple I know had purchased a home for $150,100 in 2000. Let's call them Chad and Carol. I remember the day they made the offer. On the phone, the realtor convinced them to offer the measly $100 above asking price due to a competitor buyer. The bid won.

I asked them 18 years later in 2018 how much they owed. I was shocked to learn around $100k. They both earned good salaries, Carol as pharmacist, and Chad worked his way up the corporate ladder. Together, they made a healthy wage crossing deep into the $300Ks, beyond what most would consider comfortable. By the way, if your goal is to be "comfortable," good. But chances are, you'll never be wealthy. If your goal is to be wealthy, you'll end up becoming ferociously comfortable. The game of money is played by rich people to win. They focus on opportunities It is played by others to "NOT LOSE." They focus on hurdles. We will learn how to win.

So, how could it be, almost two decades later, they still owed over 66%? The answer is simple; hidden costs of owning a home. Many financial pundits familiar with the issue, have described home ownership as the most detrimental financial decision people can make.

On a $150k loan over 30 years, accounting for the interest alone (5% is currently the national average. Although, when they bought it was around 9%), you will have paid a total of $300k. That's not a typo. Multiply the "sticker price" of your home by two, and that's true "asking" price; accounting mortgage interest alone, considering you didn't take out home equity loans (like most, you probably did). Add in a new roof every ten years, you're looking at racking on another $30k to your mortgage. But this still doesn't tell the full story.

What else would you pay double the value for knowing the hidden costs upfront? Milk is currently $3.27 per gallon. Financing a gallon over 30 years at an interest rate of 5%, the total cost would be $6.32 (I don't recommend keeping milk for 30 years). You're probably thinking you'd find an alternative to the cow. Or maybe you already pay that for the "organic" jug. But why do we accept a double price tag for something nearly 100,000 times that of milk (hint: your house)? We've been trained to ignore the hidden costs.

To bypass a bland discussion, the expense of interest, maintenance, renovations, property taxes, transactional costs, homeowner's insurance, utilities, and furnishing, among others, makes owning a home more like the home owning you. You can expect the total cost of ownership to be around ten percent of the value of your home per year. These are often labelled as phantom costs. To put that into perspective, if you own that $150,000 home, you probably aren't so lucky, expect to spend $15,000 per year of ownership as a token of such.

I was recently catching up with an old friend. He was shocked to discover I was still renting at 33 years old. He was equally surprised when he saw my investment accounts.

"^#%&@$, how are you so rich? You're not old enough to have all that money floating around!"

26

We discussed his family's new home and all the work they'd put in. Topping the list was a $65k remodel of the kitchen. They needed the gas range and granite island to UberEats their McDonald's? And plank flooring to easily clean the French fry grease the dogs didn't lick up? Kidding aside, will that "investment" pay off?

The average duration of ownership per home is 12-15 years. It's safe to say, when it's time to sell, styles will change. It's unlikely your style was even in line with the buyer. Pink bathroom fixtures anyone? If you don't believe me, watch *House Hunters* for a couple hours. Like a shiny new car, enough time will pass to deem the invested amount worthless.

Unfortunately, most people don't see the bigger picture and the cyclical behavior of remodeling continues. They take five to ten years to start building "equity," only to take out a home "equity" loan to remodel. Or better yet, for repairs. It's the only "equity" you'll ever have to pay for and makes about as much sense as taking out an equity loan on your savings account. Talk about Groundhog Day. Cheers to another 30 years of payments!

Go ahead. Talk dirty to me and tell me how your house is an investment. There are three instances where I'd attempt not to laugh. Flipping, creating rental income, or paying cash, the latter still being a poor one. Otherwise, it's the biggest liability you'll ever "own."

But the housing market is hot! Correct. But it was also hot in 2007 before the housing crisis. In my opinion, home ownership is one of the single greatest inhibitors of wealth (right next to not investing). Although your house went up in value, so did the next house you're going to buy. It will likely be a larger financial obligation. After all, now you need more space to accommodate all those toys! And don't forget all the transactional costs in between.

Yes, houses do tend to appreciate, but on the magnitude of three percent annually. With an average historical inflation rate of one to two percent, paying cash for the face value with no other costs would make breaking even a win. When you add in loan interest, or the total ten percent annual phantom costs of home ownership, using the word investment and home in the same sentence seems immoral.

So why are we taught home ownership is an investment? We are programmed from early on to shoot for the white picket fence. The truth is it is an investment. For the bank, among others, not you. In fact, investing companies pool home mortgages into shares to sell as an investment vehicle. They are call REMICS or asset backed securities. Again, more people earning at the expense of your home ownership.

Owning a home is an emotional investment. It is somewhere to watch your family grow and have lasting memories. But if you approach it blindly, it is the biggest fly trap to building wealth there is. And it follows you regardless of how high your income grows, since of course, you can now afford "more house"

Can housing prices really keep rising? Most families get locked in overwhelming payments as it is. The culprit is a growing population and limited inventory. If the price of housing continues to rise, the herd will continue to "buy." As long as banks are lending. They may eventually need to offer a "lifetime" term mortgage, but if the monthly payments are affordable, it's acceptable to most. The true cost isn't in our realm of understanding.

Is home ownership all bad? No. But if your goal is to get wealthy, make sure you calculate the true cost of ownership and weigh the pros and cons of renting versus buying. Try using a rent vs. buy calculator to help. A good one is https://smartasset.com/mortgage/rent-vs-buy.

Of course, you do need to live somewhere. If your goal is to build wealth, a better way is to build assets first. Once they appreciate faster than your lifestyle of choice costs, you can leverage them to prevent liabilities from hindering your net worth. More on that later.

Unlike a home, when you convert investments to cash, you are not required to reallocate it immediately. Although you aren't required to buy a residence either, the street isn't quite as comfortable.

If you're like me, in the greater Boston area, the above calculator deems *"Renting will always be better than buying over the length of the loan"* for most properties.

To purchase a home in my area, I'd be lucky to get a comparable shack for $450k. And it'd be quite the fixer upper. It would be a win if the ten percent annual costs of ownership applied and would run me $45k. In contrast, I can comfortably rent for around $24k. That covers all my costs, and I won't be on the street if I miss a payment. I have no lawn to mow, and even get a pool and gym out of the deal. If a career or business opportunity arises, I am easily mobile.

But more importantly, it allows me to allocate money toward faster appreciating, less restrictive assets. So, is renting a sure-fire way to build wealth? It depends on what you do with the extra money. If you think it opens your monthly allotment to get a nicer set of wheels, fat chance! Let us look at a quick calculation to drive what I am talking about home (pun intended).

Jane can afford up to $2,500 per month for housing. She is a young professional aged 23 and earns a salary of $85,000. She wants a nice place to call home but would also like to build wealth. She has saved $25,000 to potentially use for a down payment or to invest. For simplicity, she has no other expenses, takes home $5,000 monthly after taxes, and her salary and expenses remain unchanged. She expects to live at this residence for at least 5 years, but wants to calculate what her net worth might be if she stayed for 5, 10, 20, and 30 years.

She found a house listed for $250,000 and an equally appealing luxury rental for $1,250 per month, including all expenses. At first glance, the monthly mortgage and rent payments appear similar. Her friends and family are peer pressuring her toward buying since "the monthly mortgage payment is almost the same as the rent." If they are only talking about property taxes and mortgage interest, they are right! But she is fairly in tune with finances and understands there will be ten percent phantom costs involved with home ownership. She digs deeper, calculating the total monthly cost of ownership to be around $2,500. Using historical data, she estimates the home could potentially appreciate in value by 3% annually.

Jane wants to invest any additional income into a stock portfolio that, based on historical data, she anticipates could return 9% annually.

A) Renting

- Rent: $1,250 monthly
- Investing: $3,750 monthly + $25,000 initial "bolus" (pharmacists feel me?)
- Rent equity built: $0

B) Home ownership

- Monthly Mortgage + phantom costs = $2,500
- Down payment (10%): $25,000
- Investing: $2,500 monthly
- Home value appreciation: 3% annually

Net worth obtained from renting (investment accounts)

- ❖ 5 years: $318,500
- ❖ 10 years: $770,500
- ❖ 20 years: $2,500,000
- ❖ 30 years: $6,700,000

Net worth obtained from owning (home equity + investment accounts)

- ❖ 5 years: $186,500(investments) - $205,000 (owed on home) +$ 290,000 (home value) = $271,500
- ❖ 10 years: $474,000 (investments) - $150,000 (owed on home) + $335,000 (home value) = $659,000
- ❖ 20 years: $1,500,000 (investments) - $61,000 (owed on home) +$450,000 (home value) = $1,889,000
- ❖ 30 years: $4,250,000(investments)- $0 (owed) + $600,000 (home value) = $4,850,000

After just 5 years, Jane's net worth is already $50,000 higher. Like getting a year's salary as bonus (after taxes) for renting for half a decade. I would take that. After 30 years, her net worth is nearly $2,000,000 greater. 53-year-olds, if someone offered you an extra $2,000,000 on the street, would you accept? I suppose paying monthly rent, against popular belief, was not flushing money down the toilet.

In fact, you could argue the contrary. And I was even generous not accounting for the closing costs on "her" home. For most, those alone will take around two years to "pay off."

When discussing home ownership, a scene from the movie happy Gilmore replays in my head. If you haven't seen it, I envy you. If only I could erase that memory and watch it again to laugh uncontrollably. Most of us had our grandparents relay what a great deal home ownership was. Taunting how much they "made" on their house. Unless, like Gilmore's grandma, they get the boot for not paying their property taxes. "I would have, but I didn't have any money."

I could pay twice the price to get half my money back or use the saved spread from renting to invest. Personally, I'd rather take the no maintenance, predictable cost route and utilize the monetary surplus for assets with a higher return. Many will "invest" the maximum they can afford monthly in a house. They'll even build some quick "equity" in exchange for credit card debt to furnish and remodel. Only to go bankrupt, shackled with high interest debt, when the earnings stop.

Heck, if you can swing it, saddle up in mom's basement for a bit. I've contemplated buying an RV and utilizing the fitness club amenities to build wealth faster. Unfortunately, the wife and kids are not on board. Luckily, 9% investment returns will look modest after completing this book.

Campus Conundrum

If you've obtained your degree, paid your debts, and landed a great career, you can skip this and the next chapter. Or read it for fun, the choice is yours. But for most of us today, we're in debt before we get our first job.

That isn't true for all. It was a challenge for me to realize that many other career paths earn more than I do with no degree and without any loans. Working their way "up" from the bottom or building a hefty following. Technically, they should have greater earnings, managing more profit and people. But you won't find their titles listed on google as a top paying career.

Our parents rarely teach us about those careers simply because they don't know they exist. It is not what they were taught, so falls outside their realm of understanding. Adults can be stubborn too, eh?

What do parents tell their kids about money? Usually, it's similar to what they learned about money in school (money 101 anyone?). Nothing! They proceed to offer financial advice based on what they "know." But that advice got them exactly where they are today. For most, broke, and still working paycheck to paycheck at advanced age. There's an old saying: "Keep doing what you've always done, and you'll keep getting what you've always got." You can try to be right all the time, or you can be wealthy. Continue to Learn and grow outside "your way."

Your wallet will thank you. Ahead, we'll discuss what they want to tell you, but haven't figured out yet.

We need and respect trade jobs. Doctors, firefighters, teachers, etc. Without them would be a travesty. But there's another path for building wealth, often better, if successful; owning a business. But starting one can be a challenge. Over 90% fail. Maintaining a career while starting a side hustle can give you the security needed during the transition to profitability. You can also buy a franchise that gives you ownership in an established business with systems in place to reduce the work and risk of starting your own. But research for return on investment is important. Most won't have the luxury to afford these out of the gate. #Goals. There are smaller scale side hustles that are more approachable. One to note is the vending business. Vending machines are relatively cheap compared to their return on investment. Many have started, or even ended, here on the journey to wealth.

Being your own boss and succeeding can be a major win for your asset column. Luckily, with investing, you can be a business owner without the hassle of running it. Investing allows you to do so in a more approachable manner through owning the stock. You take part in dividend payments and share appreciation through earnings growth without the hard work, sweat, and tears. Aside from the work your money does for you.

And the scheduled income from a career to invest over time is an asset in itself. Getting a lump sum; lottery winnings, inheritance, etc., has been the culprit of dark days for many. Won a million dollars? A million dollars of desires awaits. In an instant, you can go right back to $0. Or worse bankrupt. Around 70 percent go broke just a few years after their big break (again, pun intended). The culprit? They do not know how to manage money. It is not taught in school. If you can't manage $1, you definitely can't manage $1,000,000. Wealthy people see every dollar as a seed that continues to be replanted. Unwealthy people see every dollar as an exchange mechanism to get what they want right now. The ability to manage the money you have determines if you will get any more. If you don't control it, it will control you.

So, is college worth it? I often question this and I'm not alone. One of the biggest political issues today is the student loan debt burden. It totals a staggering $1.5 trillion as of this writing, of which, more than 44 million Americans account for.

College can be worth it if you can justify the cost with future earnings. As a pharmacist, I was lucky to earn six figures after graduating. Demand for pharmacists was high, not so much anymore, and the degree can provide a foundation for other health professions. Education provided a relatively near-term return on my investment that is not realized with many degrees.

Most students don't have a clear career path out of the gate. This can be costly. Originally inspired to become a dentist, I changed trajectory after getting my undergrad in biology. Luckily, two of the years were relevant. After taking a few summer classes, I was able to transfer into the third of six-year PharmD program. But the two-year indecision cost me $60,000 of private tuition. Tack on interest and deferred payments over the subsequent 8 years, it accounted for $87,280/$225,000, or 38%.

It's essential to remove the blindfold when applying for a degree. Like a home, weigh the benefits of obtaining the degree in question with its cost. If you are shackled with debt and limited career opportunities upon graduation, you lose the power to choose. Aside from where to hang your framed degree (mine is collecting dust in the closet). The school will sell you the frame, too, only $100! And don't count on the government for help. They've succeeded in making forgiveness programs a complex maze. Less than 1% will qualify.

Full of Leverage

"It doesn't go down!" an all too familiar conversation with colleagues from graduate school regarding their student loans.

Student loan repayment isn't one size fits all. Paying a smaller amount monthly gives you more working capital but is also dangerous. You'll pay more over the life of the loan, thanks to interest and will give you more capital to get locked in a lifestyle that kicks your net worth in the gut.

But wait, I'm planning on using a forgiveness program. Tread carefully. Many speak highly of these, but research is crucial. And they all have one thing in common, they don't want you to qualify.

Qualifying for forgiveness is like buying a lottery ticket. Less than one percent of students get through the puzzle created by government forgiveness programs. Education departments have not helped. I'd encourage you to try, especially if you have low income or work in a qualifying industry. But the complex rules entailed may just leave you with a rejection letter, so don't count on them to save the day.

So how did I manage to tackle my loan while investing? It all starts with a vision. Financial advisors will charge you for advice to pay off debt quickly. Investment brokerages will tell you to invest early. But who's right? The answer is both, and it depends.

Paying off debt quickly feels euphoric, but what's the cost? What's the right balance between investing and paying debt? Step one is to determine the true cost of your loan, how much you can commit to investing and what are the expected returns. I'll walk you through my personal example.

I graduated several years ago, popping educational tags of $225,000. I had no cash. I was able to build up what I perceived to be a sizable chunk of change during my six-month deferral period. Unfortunately, the 7.5% interest negated my savings of $25k just as quickly.

There was a taunting rhetoric by parents and advisors to pay it off quickly, investment firms not to, and driven away from refinancing by other financial "professionals." When push comes to shove, the biggest determinant is the loan interest cost versus potential investment returns.

To simplify, there's an inflection point when your investments will grow faster than your loan is costing you. If you have a minimal amount to invest and a sizable, high interest debt burden, it pays to work on reducing the balance to manageable territory first. But what about when you are positioned better as time passes?

I went against the advice of many and refinanced with a bank called D.R.B. At the time, they gave out low interest loans for healthcare professionals. I was able to reduce my interest rate from 7.5% to 3.5%(variable) almost overnight. It didn't hurt that I had an excellent credit score and "high" salary. The risk was losing the "benefits" of federal loans and banking on my salary to continue coming in.

To be fair, federal loans do have some benefits. I won't go into detail, but the biggest are the option to defer in hardships and income-based repayment plans. These allow you to pause, or pay a capped monthly payment based on a percentage of your income. It's possible if you pay the minimum payment for the agreed term, the remainder will be forgiven after approximately twenty years. But don't get too excited, the total dollar amount will likely exceed the original face value significantly unless you have a very low income.

Some private banks aren't as forgiving, so research is paramount. But if your income is stable and high, the choice to refinance out of federal loans is a no brainer. Unless you like donating extra money to the government. Hey, bridges are a worthy cause! Some of the best lenders I've come across are earnest, citizens, and laurel road/D.R.B. They're not sure what they want to be called. A bit of an identity crisis.

I went back and forth between variable and fixed loans as the rate on variables tend to creep upward over time. Once you build enough assets to outright pay off the loan, variable is the way to go. It is a risk in that the rate can increase over time up to a cap, but you gain a lot of leverage once you acquire the ability to pay it off. That doesn't mean you should! You can also re-finance again to a fixed or lower variable rate later if your current rate implodes, or have the option pay the loan off if its sensible (Hint: it won't be if you understand the investing techniques in this book). I went from 7.5% federal loans, to 3.5% variable (D.R.B.), to 3.99% fixed (earnest), to 0.38% variable(earnest) approximately every two years. As the balance went down and my assets grew, I felt less cornered and was more comfortable with a variable rate. As your financial situation improves, continue to hunt for the lowest rate.

So how do you determine when to start investing? Warning: were going to do some heavy math. All those wasted hours in school on problems you thought you'd never need to use have prepared you for this moment. Your opportunity to build wealth. Just kidding, were going to have calculators do it for us.

We need to compare the loan balance and interest cost against our expected investment returns. The average annualized total return for the S and P over the past 90 years is 9.8%. Although this can vary greatly by year, it's a fair estimation that can gauge potential success in our calculations. We'll talk later about strategies to shatter expected returns.

Using a simple investment calculator, we can find the inflection point where our investments will earn faster than the loan interest costs. Try using[3]. Fill in a few simple fields and determine how much your investments will be worth during a selected period.

Simultaneously, utilize a basic debt interest calculator to determine how much your debt will cost you over the same period at[4].

---

[3] https://www.calculator.net/investment-calculator.html

[4] https://calculator.me/loan/

You can also review the amortization schedule to see what the balance will be at certain points in time. For me, it looked something like this:

Scenario 1: Waiting to invest until the 10-year loan is paid in full

My friend from pharmacy school gave me permission to share his "strategy."

Loan balance: $225,000.

Loan Interest: 7.5%.

Term: 10 years.

Monthly Payment: $2,670.

Total interest: $95,500.

Total amount paid: $320,500.

Net worth after five years: (-$133,300).

Net worth after ten years: Zero.

Net worth after 15 years if invested loan payment amount after paid in full: $204,500.

Net worth after 20 years if invested loan payment amount after paid in full: $533,600.

Net worth after 30 years (if invested loan payment amount after paid in full): ($1,917,700).

Scenario 2: If prolonged the loan term only and invested additional "savings."

Loan: $225,000.

Loan Interest: 7.5%.

Term: 20 years.

Monthly Payment: $1800.

Total interest: $210,000.

Total amount paid: $435,000.

Invested an additional $870 monthly.

Expected return: 10%.

Loan balance after five years: $195,500.

Investment balance after five years: $66500.

Net worth after five years: (-$129,000).

Loan balance after ten years: $152,500.

Investment balance after ten years: $173,500.

Net worth after ten years: $21,000.

Loan balance after 20 years: zero.

Investment balance after 20 years: $624,500.

Net worth after 20 years: $624,500.

Net worth after 30 years: $2,150,000.

As you can see in this example, despite the high initial loan amount, it would have been worth it to extend the term to 20 years if you committed to investing the difference. The expected net worth notably improved after the five-year mark and continued outpacing scenario one moving forward (paying the loan off in total before investing). That's the power of compound interest. Yet, even better options are realized below.

Scenario 3: If refinanced over same initial term, and invested the monthly "savings."

Loan: $225,000.

Term: Ten years.

Interest: 3.7%.

Payment: $2,250.

Monthly savings to be invested from refinancing: $420.

Total loan interest: $44,500.

Total amount paid: $269,500.

Loan balance after five years: $123,000.

Investment balance after five years: $32,000.

Net worth after five: (-$91,000).

Loan balance after ten years: zero.

Investment balance after ten years: $84,000.

Net worth after ten years: $84,000.

Net worth after 15 years if invested loan payment amount after paid in full: $338,000.

Net worth after 20 years if invested loan payment amount after paid in full: $747,500.

Net worth after 30 years: $2,500,000.

Scenario 4: If refinanced over longer term and invested additional monthly "savings".

Loan: $225,000.

Term: 20 years.

Interest: 5.5%.

Payment: $1550.

Monthly amount invested: $1,120 ($2,250-$1,550+$420).

Total interest: $146,500.

Total amount paid: $371,500.

Loan balance after five years: $189,500.

Investment balance after five years: $85,700.

Net worth after five years: (-$103,500).

Loan balance after ten years: $142,600.

Investment balance after ten years: $224,000.

Net worth after ten years: $81,400.

Loan balance after 15 years: $81,000.

Investment balance after 15 years: $446,000.

Net worth after 15 years: $365,000.

Loan balance after 20 years: $0.

Net worth after 20 years: $804,500.

Net worth after 30 years: $2,620,000.

As you can see. Refinancing resulted in a potential net worth creep of almost $500k after 30 years. If you met your 30-year older self and someone offered you $500k, would you accept? I would if they offered a $20.

Although that is the best option at the original entry position, it can improve further as your financial picture changes. The loan value will go down and assets will grow. Financial leverage is a big asset when it comes to refinancing loans. I suggest re-orienting your financial picture and trying to hunt for better rates every one to two years. Making the calculations and taking the lowest interest rate can afford you a big pay day if you invest the difference. Here's an example that would be encountered a few years down the line, utilizing above scenarios, after the balance was reduced.

Recalculating After Reducing the Balance: Future Situation

Remaining Loan amount: $112,000.

Interest rate: 3.99%.

Amount invested: $330,000.

Current monthly payment: $2,030.

Payment term: 61 months remain.

Total interest remaining: $11,927.35.

Monthly investment allotment: = $2,090

Expected investment return: 10%.

Net worth after 61 months: $692,000.

Net worth after ten years (reinvested additional payment amount moving forward after loan paid in full): $1,429,905.

Net worth after 15 years: $2,618,308.

Net worth after 20 years: $4,532,244.

Net worth after 30 years: $12,578,915.

Scenario 1: If refinanced again, extending term, and invested additional "savings."

Loan amount: $112,000.

Interest rate: 3.99%.

Amount invested: $330,000.

New monthly payment: $1,134.

New monthly investment allotment: $2,090+$896= $2,986.

Payment term: Ten years.

Total interest: $24,009.60.

Expected investment return: 10%.

Net worth after five years: $61,558.58+$760,000= $698,442.

Net worth after ten years: $1,452,728.

Net worth after 15 years: $2,655,065.

Net worth after 20 years: $4,591,441.

Net worth after 30 years: $12,732,455.

Scenario 2: If refinanced, extended payment term further, and invested additional.

Loan amount: $112,000.

Interest rate: 4.82%.

Amount invested: $330,000.

New monthly payment: $708.18.

New monthly investment allotment: $2,090+$1,322= $3,412.

Payment term: 20 years.

Total interest paid: $62,734.19.

Expected investment return: 10%.

Net worth after five years: $93,167.80 + $792,695 = $699,528.

Net worth after ten years: ($69,214.99) + $1,537,870 = $1,468,656.

Net worth after 15 years: $(38,749.27) + $2,737,982 = $2,699,233.

Net worth after 20 years: $4,670,775.

Net worth after 30 years: $12,938,226.

As you can see, extending the term to 20 years and investing the remainder made my 30-year-older self $359,311 wealthier. And that's in addition to accounting for any savings realized up to that point. Pretty impressive. Especially for a cheap date like myself.

But what if you had enough assets to pay the loan outright? Should I have just paid it off? Let's look and see how things would turn out.

Scenario 3: Just pay it off, brah!

Loan amount: $112,000.

Paid in full cash money.

Starting investing amount: $330,000.

New amount to invest monthly: $2,030+$2,090= $4,120.

New invested amount after loan paid = $330,000-$111,500= $218,500

Net worth after five years: $667,328.

Net worth after ten years: $1,390,171.

Net worth after 15 years: $2,554,317.

Net worth after 20 years: $4,429,186.

Net worth after 30 years: $12,311,608.

Paying it off felt great! But your 30-year older self is losing out on over $625k. You could have used that to outright purchase a yacht, or better yet, more assets. Not cool, dude. Technically, we could have increased our debt, while simultaneously improving our net worth potential. We would have paid more by extending the terms of the loan, yet it simultaneously afforded our investments to appreciate to a greater magnitude. This is a result of the inflection point being reached. The average investment balance and return rate was higher than the loan balance and interest rate. Hence, net worth grew.

Continue utilizing the calculators until you determine the sweet spot where investing makes sense while simultaneously attacking the debt. Most lenders will give you an estimated interest rate based on selected terms without a hard credit pull. It's not an exact science but will point you in the right direction to make a well-informed decision.

You also want to play with the time frame and payment amount. When you have little or no debt, the answer is easier. When you have a lot like I did, it pays off even more to make the calculations. Fun fact: this works for all loans. Incorporating this mindset into any type of debt will pay off. Literally!

This topic brings to light an important point. One that prevents many from building wealth. Paying debt off quickly can greatly hinder your wealth potential. Although being "debt free" makes you feel warm and fuzzy inside, it has no relation to being wealthy. Ask the richest people in the world if they are "debt-free." They will laugh. Hard. They will also call it something different: Leverage. The truth is, wealthy people understand that like salary, debt is a tool. The way you service it can make or break you.

Another trait of the rich? They think in percentages, not dollar amounts. Want an easier example? If you have $100k in assets and $100k in debt, most would just assume pay it off, right? It depends. If the assets appreciate at 10%, and the debt is serviced at 3%, that mindset could prove costly. Debt is a tool. Learn how to use it. Your net worth will thank you.

I grossly underestimated how much my investments would appreciate, making 10% estimated returns laughable. We'll dig deep into the strategies I used to enhance returns in a later chapter. Today, I still carry a small loan balance. I determined the best formula to accumulate the highest net worth based on my situation and reassess it annually.

Since my investment accounts overbear the debt burden by more than tenfold and have a higher return rate than interest rate, it would be foolish to pay it off. The assets grow at a faster rate and value than the debt costs. Like pouring fuel on a fire, that's the power of compound interest.

Living the Dream!

Given the choice between working and retiring early, most would choose the latter. Today, the majority work over 80% of our time on earth for money, all to finance a lifestyle we can afford the monthly payments for. The banks collect interest from us. The government collects 30-50% of our earnings. The rest fades into monthly payments. Under a microscope, it's financial slavery. It's easy to see why there is a heavy competition to earn more money.

Early on, I idolized people working toward high income instead of putting money to work. I watched them accumulate liabilities as earnings grew, initially making the same grave mistakes in fear of cultural inferiority.

But is shooting for a big salary all it cracked up to be? It greatly depends on what you will do with the money. Earning more income can greatly enhance your wealth potential, but can equally serve as your adversary. The wheels spin faster, but if they don't touch the ground, you still won't get very far.

The mindset of most would include using the additional "monthly" income for something like "more house." They end up falling for the greatest informercial of all time, financing the "American Dream." Just 780 easy monthly payments, that rise on a sliding scale with your salary. If that is your intention, run! You'll be working forever to keep the lights on. They repeat the cycle over and over, expecting a different result. "If I can just earn more, then I'll be rich." If your goal is to build wealth, and your intention is to utilize the extra money to invest, I approve.

When we see someone that has surface wealth, our brain immediately ponders the following thoughts: what do they do for work? How much do they make? Buying into this mindset is why many people stay broke. A better question: what does their money do? Not investing can feel like running on a hamster wheel. You remain stagnant. We'll discuss how you can build wealth first and how to leverage it to keep it growing.

Let's explore a quick calculation to drive this point home. Most people think wealth is obtained by salary, and best gauged by home size. But these are misleading metrics. There are more powerful forces at play.

Steve is a carpenter. He worked from age 18 for his dad's business earning a modest salary of $65,000. He lived at home until age 25, and was able to invest 75% of his earnings for those 7 years living at home.

His brother Simon took a different path. He worked for his father as for 1 year as well and bought a new mustang GT with most of his income. After realizing there were much better performance cars on the market (out of reach with his current salary), he decided to pursue a secondary degree.

He went to college for 6 years to obtain his master's in business. He started in the hole due to student loans, but figured he could more that justify the cost with his future salary. Despite his education, he retained a desire for the "finer things in life." Working his way through the corporate ranks, he amassed a $250,000 salary by age 35. Lifestyle creep followed suit. He continued his rock star career, and age 50 was a CEO earning $1,000,000 annually.

Both brothers went on to have a family. Although Steve admittedly lived a more modest lifestyle, he was focused on putting first things first. Namely, his family and finances. Although his salary remained stagnant, he was able to continue investing 25% after moving out of his parent's place at 25.

Simon was focused on putting his money where his mouth was. Namely, into impressive liabilities. He had all the bells and whistles but wasn't able to start investing until his big salary break at 50. He started putting 10% of his post tax earnings to work.

Fast forward to 65, here is how they fared earning the same 9% annual return.

Steve
- ❖ Net pay: $50,000
- ❖ Amount invested: 75% = $37,500 annually or $3,125 monthly x 7 years at home
- ❖ Initial 7-year portfolio balance w/ returns: $359,026
- ❖ Amount invested (age 25 and on): 25% =$12,500 annually or $1,042 monthly
- ❖ Investment balance at Age 65 = $15,673,245

Simon
- ❖ At age 50

- ❖ Net pay $600,000
- ❖ Amount invested (age 50): 10% = $60,000 annually or $5,000 monthly
- ❖ Investment balance at Age 65 = $1,833,193

The good news: you can stop envying your bosses salary! As illustrated, if you're waiting for salary alone to make you rich, I hope you enjoy life as a skeleton. There are bigger powers at play. These include time, relative frugality, and compound interest. If you build wealth first, little can stop your trajectory.

I recently had a conversation with one of my may mentors about interest in "moving up." A $50,000 promotion. I got the same old bologna, "Do my job and I'll take the credit. I'll put in a good word when something comes up."

That's far from what they said. But a whimsical attempt at telling it like it is. The hard truth is it's often "all who you know." At least for me, that puts a buzzkill on my desire to climb corporate ladders. Only to work harder, pay the taxman more, and make the company richer. All while the money whispers temptation for a lifestyle creep.

I was always envious of peers that found the formula to advance quickly and make that big promotion. I initially played that role, becoming a pharmacy supervisor from a floater within two months of obtaining my license. I even dabbled into some covering director roles and responsibilities to get my name out there.

I mimicked the path of the peers I looked up to. Diving into every leadership book, I could find and capitalizing on every opportunity to expand the parameters of my role. The results spoke loudly and my business soared. But that isn't enough in corporate America today. You need to network feverishly and be your bosses' pal. As I aged and built wealth, I grew stubborn in succumbing to office politics.

Growing up as an introvert, it wasn't quite my style. I liked being disguised like an unassuming "sleeper" (or "Q-car" if your British) packing high performance under the hood. In college, I was given the nickname "Quiet Mike," yet the entire campus knew me.

I kept pressing and put my personal finance first as an outcome that mattered in my life. I shifted my focus from making my company rich*er* to making myself rich. Anytime I got a raise or promotion, I invested the additional amount immediately into assets before I had a chance to spend it. Luckily, being frugal in that role was enough to build a portfolio that will pay me for a lifetime.

Some colleagues made it "big" taking the career path. I mentioned earlier some even had salaries crossing into the millions. Originally, finding out their salaries was depressing. My parents had told me to study hard and earn a trade degree. What they were taught was a high income. Why didn't they discuss the path to become an executive or CEO? Or to build multiple income streams?

Meet the Parents reference number two (an all-time favorite movie).

After meeting Pam's ex-fiancé, Greg and Kevin converse about their careers. When millionaire wall street investor Kevin finds out Greg's a male nurse, he responds in a way he feels relatable. Telling Greg he'd like to find some time to do some "community service" as well, recently seeing a golden retriever with a "gimp." Greg replies, "He does get paid as well but it also feels good."

Harsh, but he makes a valid point. Working for money instead of letting it work for you is leaving earnings on the table. This is exactly how I felt realizing many earned the same salary as me (I once thought was high) monthly. Google fibbed. I wanted to do something about it. Luckily, it was early enough to change my financial trajectory.

But all the big Whigs had one thing in common, they were still working. They were going big on the "American dream," or going home. The more they made, the more they spent.

A close acquaintance "owned" three houses in addition to a luxury condo in the mountains with rent that trumped my gross monthly income.Another, a slew of automotive payments that gave my annual salary a run for its money. Was it for the love of being at the office? Or was it the fear of losing the ability to make the payments of their high maintenance lifestyle?

Additionally, their personal lives struggled as big responsibilities made family life a burden. They all longed for more time and meaningful relationships, imprisoned by the fight to find happiness in materials.

Ever asked them how they are doing? They'll usually say something like "Living the dream!" It has a hint of underlying sarcasm. But it's telling. Here's what they are really saying. They are overworked and still broke. They got somewhere they aimed for, but it wasn't what they expected. The money didn't go as far as they anticipated. They are on a trajectory to work forever, with no end in sight. They are caught in the thick of thin things. That's a lot of thoughts! Don't get me started on what it means when people say "I'm well." Although grammatically correct, it hints at the level of excitement present in their life (I have to keep this a little interesting).

Earning money is just part of the equation. High income does not guarantee wealth, and has the potential to set you up for financial obligations that guarantee you work forever. The less sexy part of building wealth is relative frugality and investing a portion of your earnings.

No matter what you make, wealth is determined by how much you pay yourself first and your net worth. It takes discipline, grit, grime, and a willingness to pass on keeping up with the Joneses for a significant period. Luckily, it's rare for a second material possession of anything to make you happier.

Yet, there is a way to balance fun and finance. If you're like me, gaining assets becomes a hobby. And you'll be happier living simply, knowing you have more options than others trapped in payments they lost track of. If greed and desire for being material rich is your motivation, it can set you up for catastrophe when the earnings stop coming in. Once you build enough revenue flow to support your lifestyle of choice, you can choose to reward yourself in ways you see fit. Or like my wiser half, invest in more assets.

Before you take that promotion, take a moment to think. Will it really add any value to your life? Or will you work yourself frantically into an early grave, being miserable and totally absorbed along the way. After all, now you earn more than your peers and can easily justify spending the extra monthly allotment. There's strong evidence supporting happiness plateauing at an annual salary of $75k.

Flushing Benjamin's

Growing up, I had many bad financial examples. Most were locked in competition to prove who was the baddest of them all. They "one upped" each other, pulling into holiday parties Porsche after Porsche.

But they weren't putting their money to work. They were burying it breathing while making the banks richer. When you pull those shiny new wheels off the lot, you immediately lose 25%-35% of your "investment." Think about your car being a ticker in your portfolio. You'd probably feel torn to find your already 25% in the red on day one and it continues dwindling down onward.

A car can be a pseudo-asset if it's necessary to get you to work, make money, or utilized to create income. Think uber, TURO, or construction jobs. I wouldn't necessarily put it in your asset column in most circumstances but driving a car until it's dead can also be a liability.

One of my first cars was a Saab 9-3 Viggen (a sleeper sedan!). If you know what that is, kudos. I returned the 96' Saab 9-3 my parents gifted me thinking I deserved a faster alternative. After taking a ride in my uncle's Viggen at our family camps in the Adirondacks, I made it my life mission to get one. Years later, I located one on *saabnetnet.com* in

Vermont and quickly contacted the "dealer." Looking back, it was more of a rundown gas station. I remember getting the call and being lured in, "I know 93,000 sounds like a large number of miles, but it's an amazing machine."

My best friend and I drove out to Vermont carrying $10,000 cash, idiotically like most things those days, waving it at bystanders like we were millionaires. Luckily, we didn't get robbed and made it home safely with the car.

Thanks to my parents, I had no payment. A feat worthy in itself and I didn't need to read Trump's "art of the deal" to negotiate. More on that later. It was necessary to get me to work. But being a 2000 in 2008 with high miles, the car came with a lot of baggage. It didn't help that it was foreign, being notoriously more expensive to repair. The car always itched to have its engine light on. During my last six months of ownership, I averaged around $500 per month in repairs. Getting something newer with a higher payment and warranty would've saved me money.

Why am I talking about cars? 1) I like them, 2) despite popular belief, you don't need to axe your daily Starbucks to be frugal. Start looking for savings within your top three expenses. For most, those are housing, transportation, and food (although for fellow pharmacists #1 is likely student loans ☹).

Cars are rarely an asset, but most of us rely on some type of transportation to make money. There is a formula of sorts that helps you reduce depreciation rate and unexpected expenses. Buy reasonably priced cars with low maintenance costs, one to two years old with less than 15,000 miles, and existing warranty. Owning several vehicles, I also utilize them to create rental income on TURO. Keeping the cars for three to four years, they still have solid value when I sell and restart the process, securing a low cost of ownership. On the other hand, buying new luxury cars to impress the Joneses tend to go in the quickly gone and forgotten column of liabilities (aside from some rare collectables that may be considered investments). Leasing is also a sure-fire way to burn cash.

But how else can you bury money? Saving generally gets a good reputation. But I'll spill the beans. Savings accounts have their place and I'd encourage anyone to hold some wealth in cash or savings. We'll discuss amounts later.

Let's explore a close role model of mine growing up. We'll call her Frugal Faith. She despised spending money, and to this day, her closet resembles what you'd find in a prison cell. Growing up as a sibling of seven, resources were sparse, and it taught her military like financial habits. She was blessed to have a high degree of satisfaction with very little.

She'd drive cheap cars into the ground and always find a way to pinch pennies. I recall many overnights at her house, getting bombarded most mornings in the bathroom, "Five-minute showers, guys, five-minute showers."

Night wasn't any safer, charging in to switch the faucets off while my sister and I brushed our teeth. I rarely used her bathroom unless an emergency arose, as I knew the toilet would be primed (she'd rarely flush). I remember heavy blanket filled winter nights as the thermostat was secured in her room, locked on 65 degrees

Her husband would jack it up when she was out, and I have a space heater on speed dial when we visit. Don't tattle, or I may get an invoice.

But why am I telling you all this? She'd built sizable savings and retirement accounts, but was she wealthy? Yes and no. She'd mastered a necessary piece of the wealth building puzzle, but she was leaving earnings on the table. At age 65, she still had the need to work and be frugal. Those should be the golden years. Saving is essential to building an emergency fund when turmoil approaches. Lost jobs, health scares, we've all been there. I'd suggest saving at least three to six months of annual salary to plan for the unexpected.

When my first son was born, my wife had a rough pregnancy. After visiting relatives for thanksgiving, she had severe vomiting and weight loss that put her into the hospital. Our initial thought was food poisoning. 30 days and 30 pounds later, she was diagnosed with Crohn's disease. Living on one income for over three months, we were glad to have a healthy savings reserve.

Yet, saving is not an avenue to build wealth. It'd be a miracle to find a bank that offers more than a two percent yield nowadays. If you do, you're likely to be ridden with restrictions and penalties for withdrawing it when you need to. So what's the cost of saving too much?

Let's look and see how saving compares to investing over a lifetime. We'll follow two individuals with the same salary that get serious about their finances at age 22 and check their account balance at age 65. Let's save some time and assume the ostentatious spenders are broke, regardless of income. If you need to learn more about that, read the book *Rich Dad, Poor Dad.*

A. Frugal Faiths high yield savings.

Starting amount: $10,000.
Yearly yield (interest, dividends, share appreciation): 1.5%.
Monthly contributions: $1,000.
Accumulated balance at age 65: $527,408.39.

B. Wealthy Wendy's personal portfolio.

Starting amount: $10,000.
Yearly yield (interest, dividends, share appreciation): 10%.
Monthly contributions: $1,000.
Accumulated balance at 65 y/o: $3,019,405.17.

Over the last century, stocks have risen and fallen. No matter how you slice it, the historical average annual return of the stock market has been around ten percent. Although the markets have proven to pack a heavy punch in building wealth, anything can happen in the near term. Allocating any money into the markets that you need in the next five years can prove dangerous. Consider any money entered as bills paid to yourself, locked for the long haul. If you invest any money you'll need to cover expenses, you're asking for trouble.

In the calculation, the only variation was the potential annual return. You just witnessed the power of compound interest. From the same starting line, with identical contributions, it's clear Frugal Faith should have flushed. Technically, she did. $2,500,000 large.

Of course, some wise girl will say, "10% yield on average is unrealistic!" They are right. With the strategies ahead, it's far too low. But there's much more to the story. If you don't understand how simple it is, you will get mediocre results at best. You can even "lose your shirt." Not to worry, well discuss how to keep it, and even layer up to a sweatshirt and jacket.

Although being frugal is helpful in the journey to wealth, making the choice to put your money to work is what's needed to break the ice. It takes putting fear aside and giving your money optimal time and opportunity to grow. But frugality, high earnings, and multiple revenue streams can speed up the process.

Again, it's unnecessary to completely axe small purchases. Think bigger. Do you really need that bigger car or house payment? Do nicer cars or bigger home expenses feed your soul more than financial freedom? Before I had a "pot to piss in," I was arrogant with spending. As I learned more about money, my mind started calculating how much every dollar I spent could be invested, and the potential balance if locked up for twenty years to life with compound interest. Thousands of decisions like that add up.

Start with the "big rocks" and make a strategic financial plan. Set your allotments for investing and pay them first, directly from your paycheck. Don't give yourself the opportunity to overspend. When you see your account balance growing, you may just fall in love with financial freedom.

"But I want to enjoy my life while I'm young, too!"

We'll discuss how to balance your personal portfolio and retirement accounts to enjoy your time during the process. It doesn't involve hiring a financial advisor. Almost 50% have no retirement plan themselves. The content in this book will help you have your cake and eat some along the way, too, if you want to.

Those that fall short of financial freedom tend to think differently. They rationalize a choice must be made between money OR happiness. They limit their potential by asking questions like do I want to have a successful career, OR great family relationships? Do I want money OR meaning? They convince themselves that money is not important, and consequently don't accumulate wealth. Those who have succeeded financially look for ways to creatively achieve "all of the above." We will discover a way to transform that OR to AND.

Hire Your Money

I'd be remiss not to dedicate a chapter on prioritizing what's important in life. If money is your only motivation, get used to always feeling poor. But who am I to decide for you? I'll simply lay the foundation for periodically confirming you are on the right track.

When I ask people what matters to them most, their answers are similar. They'll relay something like: family, health, finances, faith, leisure, etc. But they rarely have enough time to engage in what matters most. They are too busy working to pay for a lifestyle, packaged into a payment they can afford monthly. As income grows, bills follow suit. We are constantly conditioned to believe that once we earn more and have nicer "things" we will be happy. It becomes normal to work forever to "pay them off."

My list is no different, including family, faith, health, fitness, charity, entertainment, and wealth, in that order. I'd encourage anyone reading to make a list of the most important things in your life and a subsequent "stewardship agreement" containing the *process goals* to help you get there. Continually develop the process goals when you learn what behaviors have the greatest impact. Here's what my personal stewardship agreement looks like for building wealth.

Wealth:

- Brainstorm and explore new investment opportunities daily.
- Limit unnecessary purchases and budget appropriately for essentials, paying particular attention to the "big three" (Housing, transportation, food)
- Leverage debt and credit strategically to maximize investment returns
- Cook meals weekly and limit dining out.
- Contribute 35% of my earnings to investment accounts directly from paycheck.
- Rebalance portfolio and cash reserves based on market conditions, in line with planned allotments yearly in a tax efficient manner.
- Maintain a manageable portfolio of up to 100 stocks (much less is appropriate initially).
- Invest along a sliding scale, more during days or periods the market or security in question is down.
- Sell only during days or periods the market or security in question is up, or if clear you were wrong and can realize losses tax efficient manner.
- Invest in a variety of stocks and sectors you know and understand.

- Hold a sliding scale of cash reserves to take advantage of market turmoil and new opportunities, up to an appropriate proportion (discussed later) and based on the current landscape (i.e. stocks are high more cash; stocks are low less cash).

- Refrain from "hype" or investing in anything your uncomfortable holding for less than five years (With the exception of clear, strategic swing trading opportunities in small, measured amounts). Manage risk in a manner where losing the entire investment creates low impact.

- Be financially, mentally, and strategically prepared to capitalize during market turmoil and overreactions, investing along a "sliding scale"

- Refrain from, or limit day or swing trades to one to two percent value of total portfolio, or amounts you are comfortable losing.

- Have a side hustle that impassions you, creating multiple streams of income (mine are adding value to others through writing and consulting)

- Build and maintain emergency savings account that covers three to six months of essential expenses.

- Calculate net worth quarterly to ensure you're on the right track.

Plan to rate yourself weekly in line with the points of your agreement. You can pick the scale, but one to ten works just fine for each section. Set aside time each week on your calendar for reflection. What is one thing you can improve on, and what steps will you take to capitalize on that opportunity moving forward? Seek advice from people with more experience if you need to.

Focus on the lessons, not the losses. Learning with real money is a big chunk of the process. Every mistake is an opportunity for growth. The most essential trait of a good investor is that they generate more cash than they consume. They continue putting that cash to back to work. In the long run, their portfolio most certainly will grow, regardless of what the stock market does. But there's more to the story.

Burning Copper

The conversation with most about investing starts something like this: "I wanted to talk to you about some stocks I bought a while ago that I'd like to sell to buy something else." Well then, why did you buy them in the first place? Do you not like them, or have you succumbed to the current mood of the share price? Will we be having the same conversation in a few months with a different security? Yes, we will. Not to worry, I have been there too! If you think you will feel differently about a company if the share price drops, you may want to reconsider buying it.

Has a similar mindset caused you to be unsuccessful at investing so far? You're not as dumb as you think. Most beginners start out inadvertently becoming a trader. They buy when markets go up and sell when the go down. This behavior of "following the market" has proven over time to hinder gains. It's important to harness the emotional framework needed to do the opposite. Buy more during times of doom and gloom and consider selling a portion when optimism returns.

My first investment experience was with penny stocks in 2004. Spongetech, C.T.I.C., AMNE. I relied on Yahoo! forums to get most of my information. The stocks were volatile and a few times, I made out big for an 18-year-old with a $100 weekly paycheck. Until I got burned.

I bought into some hype about a company called American green group (it traded under the tag AMNE). I'd witnessed similar stocks explode and was confident this would be no different.

Deciding to take a risk, I invested all I had all at once. The rug was pulled beneath my feet. As quick and inexplicable as a nosebleed, the stock went to zero in days. At the time, it felt like a tragedy. But it made me hungrier than ever to learn the game.

Luckily at 18, I didn't have much to my name but a couple grand. People with a fixed mindset would have let this be the end. I'll just save and continue to punch the clock. Luckily, I had one of growth. I focused on the lesson, not the loss.

Here's what I learned. Don't follow the hype, or you may find yourself searching google for a "business" with images of an abandoned building and weed filled parking lot. Bitcoin anyone? To be fair, there may be something there. But don't put all your eggs in one basket.

A few of my relatives have recently asked me about companies that are manufacturing covid-19 testing devices or vaccines. After the share prices have soared, they are thinking about burrowing in to build a position. But by the time the general public knows about it, it's typically too late, and you may be left holding the bag. These were generally unknown or forgotten companies that rose due to a special circumstance. Falling into hype after the summit is usually a surefire way to get burned. As we will discuss, it's rarely a good idea to roll with large allocations, and best reserved for the trading crowd. Have you had a bad investing experience in the past? Channel your hippocampus, and think back. Wine a little inside and say "I was such a moron!" Now, let it go. That is not serving you today.

Before we move onto the next chapter, please review the summary below of all the reasons you should not invest.

Cash Is Queen

Now that the boring part is over, let's get to talking about how to shatter expected investment returns. It doesn't involve following advice from financial articles or analyst price targets. If they were true stock genies, they wouldn't be working for median income.

Analysts, market writers, and TV hosts have many things in common. They have better odds of predicting the weather than making accurate stock targets. They are wrong over 70% of the time. When the stocks don't perform and prices drop, their price targets and articles follow suit. They are letting us know about the nor'easter after we've already shoveled the driveway. Another commonality, they're still working. Their career is a misnomer. Point being most things they say are hot air to get higher ratings and more clicks. Their job is to make reporting the market drama filled and sexy. It isn't.

To be fair, there are good analysts and bad analysts. Filtering them out is similar to picking winning stocks. Although some excel at their trade, they are under considerable pressure to manage risk for stakeholders under their "house rules." I would argue they often do so over focusing on potential investment returns. Many growth animals or industry disruptors fail to meet their inclusion criteria, and they are prohibited from making new money commitments. The result? They end up missing the boat. Since screening and risk standards limit their access to certain securities, the process is often automated to honor risk obligations of stakeholders at the cost of returns. They end up being their own enemy. If they match or beat the benchmark, they are content with keeping their job.

On the other hand, street published analysts are mostly plain old wrong. It's no secret forecasts are suspect at best. If you inspect ratings of any individual security, you will find that both bulls and bears coexist. But they are reporting the short-term emotional sentiment of the investment vehicle in question, rather than the true underlying value. I.e. when a stock underperforms the benchmark, the rating transitions to sell and vice versa. If you are a contrarian to that rhetoric in some magnitude, it can serve you very well. With regard to risk, there are better ways to mitigate it than detailed inspections during a snapshot in time with unknown variables. By the time the report is complete, the music has changed. But they do have some utility. People actually listen to them in the short term. This can present opportunities to capitalize on near misses. Onward.

A popular television host has talked about how cash can be king in some of his books, and he's partially right. I'm not suggesting you watch him or take his advice. To me, cash is queen. In the game of chess, the King is rigid. He, like the overall market, is at the leisure of the rest of his pieces with little control over the direction of the competition. In himself, he offers low impact. The nature of the game itself is unpredictable to him. The Queen is pliant with the ability to change the outcome of the game. She has utility under varying conditions. When things are good, she has the luxury to be more conservative. If things turn south, she can adjust her strategy to modify the outcome the game.

Leaving money off the table risks missing out on gains and compounded interest. But there's a key strategy that's rarely talked about in any financial text I've come across. More on that soon, but I never regretted having cash on hand to take advantage of market volatility and opportunities that arose.

On the same token, fund managers will often label cash as "trash." After all, you can't earn from money not invested! Partially true, but that assumes you will be right 100% of the time. Being "all-in" leaves you in checkmate when the experts change their mind on the direction of markets. Is it coincidence, the more cash they have under management, the more they earn? To date, 2020 was one of the worst performing years on record for funds, compared to their benchmark (while several sectors rocketed). People pulled cash from funds at historic rates. I think they are finally starting to catch on. The truth is "trash" turns to gold when the storm arrives. When the markets crash, you should deploy cash!

My suggestion is to keep cash on the order of 15-40% of your portfolio based on your age and current market conditions. That baseline scale can vary based on your individual risk tolerance. Some may even decide to have nothing in the market when we're flying high. To be clear, the intention is not to "time" the market, but to limit risk exposure and enhance returns. Afterall, 60-85% of your portfolio would still be live. Some wise girls will say, but holding cash invites inflation to reduce its value. That is ridiculous and suggests that markets go directly up without ever taking a breath. If you check into history, you'll find that is never the case. There is a greater power. I call it "inflated cash." When stocks go on sale, cash becomes worth more as the potential appreciation of investments rises with new money commitments, regardless of the cost of goods.

A sliding scale of cash has similar utility to the queen in chess. When markets are breaking all-time highs, it feels great! Our gut tells us to invest more! It also tells us to eat more when were already full (that usually doesn't turn out well either). But history tells us euphoria will eventually run out. Being apprehensive during these times is merited. If you have no cash during corrections, you are missing the boat for the next cycle. For me, it is time to strategically take some profits and reallocate funds toward cash reserves, up to 25%.

On the flip side, markets can turn on a dime. Before you know it, you'll be humming Billy Ellishes "the party is over." When big money decides to flow out, algorithms are working hard to limit losses, often creating a sell off and disrupting the supply and demand of securities. When you feel physically ill, like doomsday is approaching, it's time to deploy the strategically placed cash reserves. During times like this, you may even decide to go "all in," depending on your personal risk tolerance.

Since the beginning of time, pessimists always have debuted from the woodwork when things get bumpy. They'll say silly things like:

"I am short XYZ!"

I am "hedging against..."

"Doomsday has arrived!"

"I told you so!"

"Shrinking economy...wages...inflation...interest rates!"

It may seem like they have some near-term merit, and offer them some temporary self-preservation. But there's one problem with their argument long term. Optimistic bulls have more money.

The key here is, you need to have the funds and courage to buy more and reduce your average share price of positions when prices are slashed. This can be due to general market fluctuations, temporary headwinds for a specific security, or special circumstances like changes in taxation. It doesn't mean you are fearless, but you embrace those feelings and do what is necessary anyway. It will never be perfect, but position scaling both in and out are great strategies we will discuss in depth later.

When markets go up, your portfolio value will rise, causing your cash scale ration to be reduced by nature. This is the time to build it back up to an appropriate percentage by strategically taking gains. The opposite holds true when markets drop. Now that your cash scale ration is higher than you'd like, it's time to deploy reserves.

Sounds[5] a bit like timing? In "The Intelligent Investor[6]," Ben Graham claims "timing is nothing." He goes on, $1 held without selling from 1966-2001 would be worth $11.71 vs. "getting out" of stocks before the "5 worst days of each year," $1 would be worth $987.21. He theorizes, however, that no one can know this until after the fact. And he's right. Big but, if you have cash ready to deploy, it's like being able to "figure out," or at least be ready for the worst days in advance.

As an example, Pete considers himself an intelligent investor and currently has a $100k portfolio. The markets seem to be breaking all time highs daily. Although the euphoric feeling seems like its everlasting, he's a realist. He does not want to miss out on additional gains but understands that markets rarely take a direct route up. Like a new England spring, the weather can change without warning.

Over the past year, his live portfolio has returned a cool 100%. He originally had $45k invested with $10k in cash reserves, or 22%. That $10k cash reserve pool has now been demoted to 10% of the value of his portfolio. He decides to pull out another $10k at strategic points, leaving $80k live with a total of $20k in cash reserves.

This is beneficial in two ways. If the markets threaten to fall, he will be geared up to deploy and turbo charge cash. If the markets continue their trek upward, he will still make

---

[5] https://mannhowie.com/youtube-valuation

[6] from the book the intelligent investor by Benjamin graham revised 2003 edition with new commentary by jason zweig page 179

money and will continue pulling out cash reserves (in a tax efficient manner) to an appropriate percentage, welcoming downward momentum.

Six months forward, Pete notices the overall market has retracted 40%. Being well diversified, his live positions only dropped 30% in value to $56k. Due to his cash holdings, his portfolio is valued at $76k for a total "loss" of 24%. He starts deploying his cash reserves responsibly. Although he understands the market could drop further, he feels safer scaling in at lower levels in places he previously wished he had a more robust position. Ten months later, the markets have recovered to prior levels and his portfolio stands at 5% cash, 95% stocks. However, his portfolio is now worth $135k due to strategically reallocating his cash reserves during turmoil.

Again, he recognizes that for safe haven, he'd like to redistribute his portfolio to an allocation of 22% cash reserves and 78% live in a tax efficient manner over the next several months. He utilizes the appropriate tax lots, and reserves sale of newer lots he accumulated until at least 12 months and 1 day after acquired them.

The moral here is, Ben Graham is right. At face value, you can't time the market. At least with all your holdings. But you can be an intelligent investor, recognizing although you can't predict the future, you can prepare to make moves in either direction beneficial. When things are going great, the probability of them getting even better slowly reduces. When they get rocky, the probability of turning the corner improves. This style of investing makes any market fluctuation a win. Below, I have included my maximum cash scale suggestions based on age. Keep in mind, you are the boss. Assign an amount that agrees with your risk tolerance.

Age 0-20 → 15%
Age 21-30→ 20%
Age 31-40→25%
Age41-50→30%
Age 51-60→40%
Age 60+ → 50%

Now that you've secured your cash reserves, put your hand over your heart and say "Dear Mrs. Market. I dare you to fall. Or continue rising. Either way, it benefits me!"

If I had a choice between two money managers with the following credentials, and same fee structures, I would choose Sarah with an "h." It would serve me well in the long run (although I'd likely spell her name wrong a lot).

A) **Mark**
  - Memorized every financial metric and formula ever created
  - Follows analyst guidance
  - Talks about complex market indicators like inflation, deflation, and interest rates
  - Uses technical analysis to identify trends
  - Says "cash is trash"

B) **Sarah**
  - Less investment experience
  - Emotional intelligence of a dolphin. A contrarian to analyst guidance

- Understands risk mitigation strategies and probabilities
- Understands cash's utility, and invests along a sliding scale

Tipping the Scale

Many beginner investors pull the trigger too quickly, getting excited by hype when things are good. It's not until they go sour, they realize they made a foolish mistake. But a sour patch for a good company is the queen's forte. Like a shark, she patiently waits to prey. Sopping up the shares cheaply, she's exposing what the market has overplayed and underpriced. She's willing to wait out the storm and enjoy the sunshine when the clouds clear.

My father asked me recently how much he needed to invest today to get rich, I couldn't help but laugh. Curious as to how I was able to build wealth so "quickly," he mustered a battery of questions. Did I get an inheritance? Win the lotto? Buy the right stock? Which stock could he buy today to get rich? How much did he need to invest? The answer wasn't sexy, and he was asking the wrong questions. The "flight plan" to building wealth isn't that simple or quick. If you're lucky, it's filled with lots of turbulence. Investing all you have at once is like boarding an airplane without a pilot.

Rarely when purchasing a stock for the first time, will it be for the cheapest price you will see over the next 6-18 months. The strategy to invest along a sliding scale mitigates the risk of paying too much. Will there be times that's not the case? Yes, and we'll chat later how to prevent missed opportunities based on risk levels. But most cases, you'll be glad you dipped your toes in slowly, avoiding the shock of the ice-cold water.

So, what's a sliding scale? Diabetic patients that inject insulin often have sporadic glucose levels after they eat. The doctor prescribes a varying number of units to inject based on their measured blood glucose levels to adequately bring down their sugar. If it stays too high for too long, organ failure, like kidney damage, or loss of vision can ensue.

So, what's this have to do with investing? It's an inverse analogy to demonstrate the benefit of investing more money when the share price drops, and less when the share price rises. If the market stays too high for too long, the consequences are less severe. But if your exposure is too high, you will likely miss out on opportunities to turbo charge cash reserves.

Investing along a sliding scale will keep your average share price lower and afford you more shares to realize gains on when things turn around. Correctly executed, it will ensure you are successful more frequently while limiting your risk. You should be grateful for red days and dread green days, because building a top-notch portfolio that shatters the market depends on volatility.

To summarize, if the share price appreciates, you make money! If it doesn't initially, you get a cheaper price and improve your margin of safety. Like stretching a spring, you improve the securities potential energy. This does not work out perfectly for every position, but greatly improves your odds of success. Later we'll discuss where diversity and asset allocation come into play, but having a position building strategy to scale into positions is an excellent way to reduce risk. It will be constructed specifically based on the asset type in question and its respective volatility, which we will cover in detail later.

Over the past 100 years, the Dow Jones index has had a negative yearly return 30 out of 100 times, or 30%. Despite that, the average return over the same period was over 8%. Twelve of those years it was down over 15%, and three down over 30%. If you only invested, or invested more along a sliding scale, during down turns, your yearly average would be much higher. [7]

So, if you invest more on days the market or security in question is down, or during periods of correction, how can't you beat the market? The average annual market returns include both red and green days, as well as bull and bear markets. You could invest irresponsibly without a strategy and still lose big, but we'll chat in detail about building a portfolio that takes advantage of turmoil and weathers rocky markets. In fact, if the road wasn't rocky, you wouldn't have the potential to make as much money!

Let's discuss a specific example to bring this point home. Like the queen, I monitor hundreds of stocks to seek out potential opportunities. One such example was Teva Pharmaceuticals. One day, I noticed the stock was getting hammered to the likes of 25% in the red. Not originally intending to make it part of my portfolio, I slowly became more intrigued. Eventually, I dipped my toes in with some cash reserves and bought a few shares.

---

[7] https://tradingninvestment.com/stock-market-historical-returns/

I often talk to potential investors about my initial set of buys being a reference point to more closely track the stock. Buying a small amount, I am hopeful the stock will continue falling, and it fell big. Setting your buy targets, especially on risky assets, is essential to mitigating your risk and locking in big future gains. But it greatly will depend on the type of asset class and risk profile of the security you are buying. More on that soon. As the stock continues to drop, you set estimated targets for when you'll pull the trigger next to build the position. If the share price drops and targets are met, the dollar amount and number of shares you purchase should increase accordingly.

I know what you're thinking. Are you nuts? Do you want me to lose all my money? The stock could go to zero, but if it's part of a balanced portfolio, one cracked egg in the dozen won't prevent us from making a tasty omelet. Later we'll discover more about the strategies needed to carefully manicure our risk. But, remember, we are rarely buying anything we don't know or understand. Nor anything we would plan on holding for less than five years, although we will touch on day and swing trading briefly later.

Would you really want a stock to be a rock star out of the gate, and guarantee paying 40% of your earnings to Uncle Sam when you sell? Nursing many positions that build generational wealth over time is a better approach; Uncle Sam has enough money.

Check out my children's book *The Wealthy Wombat*.

If you foresee any scenario of a company going belly up within five to ten years, you should be reluctant to consider owning it for a second.

We'll also cover in detail how diversification can prevent one sour position from denting your portfolio. But for now, Teva. Teva was a stock I knew and understood as a pharmacist, but initially didn't see value in the share price. When it started dropping, I felt I had a first-class ticket to a ride in a time machine. A large cap company had transitioned to a period of distress. These types of assets have a different, shorter term utility that we will cover later on.

I knew their business had accounted for around 80% of generic drugs nationwide and generics were not going out of style any time soon. Many people depend on them, like water, for survival and the aging population is only growing. They also can formulate complex generics like biologics, a claim to fame not many other generic companies can' match (durable competitive advantage, if you will).

I had caught a good company during a bad time. Ridden with generic competition, patent expirations, and opioid lawsuits, the share price went on clearance. At one point, it was trading at a price to earnings ratio of one vs. its industry average of 75. Could it have gone bankrupt? Possibly, but the business plays an integral role in the pharmacy industry which would cause turmoil for patients. A government bailout or competitor buyout would be more likely if the market cap got cheap enough. Let's look at what my portfolio dashboard looked like while building that position.

Buy 1: 35 shares @ $23.85 (Ouch).
Buy 2: 52 shares @ $20.85.
Buy 3: 64 shares @ $18.73.

Buy 4: 68 shares @ $17.56.

Buy 5: 119 shares @ $16.62.

Buy 6: 94 shares @ $16.08.

Buy 7: 79 shares @ $ 11.86 (Is it still dropping?).

Buy 8:123 shares @ $9.64.

Buy 9: 134 shares @ $8.86.

Buy 10: 143 shares - $8.35.

Buy 11: 142 shares - $ 7.72.

Buy 12: 155 shares - $7.06.

As you can see, as the share price continued to drop, I accumulated more shares at the lower price. In the Teva example, this allowed most of my shares to be acquired cheaply, forced the average share price down, and mitigated my risk. The shares did see-saw in between my buys, at one point going back to $26 from a low of $11. At that point, I decided to remove the principle of my position to eliminate my risk exposure. I also took some additional profits as the position grew larger than I was comfortable holding, based on my planned allocation percentage. I was lucky in two ways. I was able to take the profit while simultaneously rebalancing my portfolio and the stock dropped again from $26 to $6 several months later. I started rebuilding my position along new targets as the allotment shrunk below my target allocation.

So how do you pick those targets? It depends on a few factors we will cover soon. One is the type of asset class. Sometimes, the historical yearly data can give some clues. For a distressed asset like Teva, the 52-week range didn't offer any assistance as it blew below support levels. It became more of a judgment call, where I selected a potential low target of $5 per share.

If I had entered my full position on the initial drop, I'd probably have a different wife today. I convinced her to invest with our wedding money. It's impossible for any stock genie to predict the bottom, but if you believe in the business and stick to the strategy, eventually things will turn around. And they turned big.

Entering your entire position at once is like buying a lifetime supply of chicken at the supermarket. Although it may seem like a good idea, it is bound to get spoiled. Instead, periodically picking up your chicken will ensure it's fresh and safe to consume. You'll likely even take advantage of some sales along the way.

If you're lucky, it will take at least a year for positions in the building stage to transpire, so you can benefit from the long-term capital gain tax advantages should you decide to sell a portion. It's easier said than done when money is burning, but this is how you will build the most successful positions. Having a well-diversified portfolio and adding or trimming positions in response to big swings will keep things in perspective and prevent any catastrophic damage.

You can also choose to purchase the same dollar amount of a stock over planned blocks of time, for example weekly, monthly, or quarterly. This is known as Dollar-cost averaging. No matter where the price heads, you'll purchase the same dollar amount, allowing you to get more shares for your money when the price is low, and less when the price is high. I often will use this strategy as a crutch for lower risk assets. If my original purchasing strategy can't be completed in a timely fashion (6-12 months), due to continued price appreciation, I'll use Dollar-cost averaging to further build a position up to the planned allocation percentage. In that manner, there's less chance of losing out on gains and while still benefiting from fluctuations. Better to take on a little caution than a lot of regret.

However, in my experience, planning targeted buys to build as the share price drops and letting the position ride as it rises, it is more effective than initially starting with Dollar-cost averaging. It also takes more patience. Your risk of heavy losses is reduced, especially with distressed or high-risk stocks. There's a low possibility you can miss out on gains, but you can always choose to dollar cost average for key positions if the planned scale isn't panning out. Later, we will talk about how the buy target scale changes based on the type of asset we are allocating funds too.

The Market Outlets

Why do markets drop? One culprit is money managers. When the markets go up, people are excited to deploy cash to into funds. After all, look at those returns! Money managers are forced to buy high, pushing the prices still higher!

As markets drop, investors start asking for their money back. Those "all-star returns" aren't looking so good anymore! Money managers are forced to SELL. So...can you do better than the "pros;" buying high, and selling low? YES!

Another reason markets move is support and resistance levels, which reflect the current supply and demand of equities. Support is where buying is ample enough to prevent further price drops. Resistance is where selling activity inhibits the security in question from rising further. But these can change on a dime with a breath of good or bad news.

People love to debate about the direction the market is heading. Common rhetoric includes talk of Interest rates...bond yields...technical analysis...bubbles...etc. Admittedly, I have NO IDEA, and I could not care less.

Knowledge of this ignorance is a superpower in markets. I'm a buyer either way. If they go up, I'll strategically capture gains for my cash reserves bank. If they go down, I have my shopping cart on speed dial.

To add an element of perspective, buying stocks cheap is like having a pair of Nikes you like go on sale. Yes, I own Nike stock as well. Nowadays, it's a challenge to find a body without some article of Nike's apparel. An analog userbase! Wouldn't you get excited if a product you've been eyeing was marked down 50%?

Imagine you walk into the Nike store. Excited to buy the new "Air's," you've saved up the $199 required. Walking to the display, Eureka! Only one pair left in your size. They are just beautiful! What will Susie think? You try them on. Like a glove. You can't hold back the smirk as you trek to the register. The associate rings them up and mentions that the price just dropped 50%. You think, oh no! I am getting more for my money. I would have much rather paid full price! Said no one ever. Yet, this is the mindset we have in the stock market.

When you buy that pair of shoes, you immediately lose a percentage or all your investment. The difference with stocks is most do not depreciate, they have a habit of appreciating significantly over time.

When buying stocks, you want to take an outlet mall or "buy your boots in the summer" approach.

Last summer, I swiped up a fancy pair on clearance for $12.99 at Burlington coat factory. It was all that much better getting compliments over Christmas (and I had a few extra dollars to deploy from Santa). Point is, we are constantly looking for undervalued opportunities that the market is missing.

My ears bleed listening to pundits tell their followers not to buy "losers." Buying losers can be key to winning big, if part of the right strategy. In fact, here is a secret. Most of my biggest gainers were once LOSERS! How you build into new and existing positions is key to enhancing returns. In some cases, it can even MAKE or BREAK you. Check out a few of my biggest "losers" that eventually turned the corner in massive fashion:

Tilray: ▼70% ⟶ ✚1000%

Wayfair ▼60% ⟶ ✚650%

Snap: ▼50% ⟶ ✚900%

Tesla: ▼45% ⟶ ✚2000%

Zillow: ▼40% ⟶ ✚450%

Disney: ▼30% ⟶ ✚220%

Ahead, we will learn how to build key positions through turmoil (or not), and how to retain your gains. All while limiting risk and reserving upside potential. Sounds too good to be true right? It's not!

To this point, I hope I've driven home; we aren't getting deep into our full position out of the gate. We are consistently investing over time, taking advantage of discounts along the way for solid companies, likely to be around for the long haul.

Imagine this. You turn on the radio and come across a financial news station called "the market outlets." Instead of the typical gloomy forecast, a pundit named Kim Lamer is happy to report that the markets are crashing. What a nice surprise! We can now buy the shares of solid companies for pennies on the dollar. In fact, she is recommending viewers sell their house, cars, and valuables to take advantage of all the bargains. "Refinance and extend the terms on your loans, were going to be rich faster than we thought!" Sound familiar? I did not think so.

Building new positions, we need to be comfortable being down, and should actually crave it. Get to the point where you're agitated when the stock rises, because we weren't finished building our position. In fact, being down more than half on risky assets should bring joy to your heart. This is the strategy in investing that gives your portfolio; "the X factor" needed to trounce market returns. A sour position for someone else may be a new opportunity for you, and the train only waits at the station for so long.

But there's a fine line between a dog and a silver horse. Continued research and intuition are necessary in deciding to continue building or to pull the plug and stop the bleeding. The answer won't always be clear. Like a multiple-choice test, go with your gut and don't change your answer. If you appropriately mapped out your plan and portfolio allocations, you will succeed regardless of the outcome.

Some things you should consider when starting new positions are:

- What's the potential risk of the asset in question?
- What is the anticipated total percentage of the security in my portfolio? And, how long do I anticipate it will take to build it?

- Am I comfortable holding for at least five years? What are the chances of it being around in ten years?
- What's the 52-week low and how much further could you foresee it falling past that (if you don't think the 52-week low is possible, you've got another thing coming)?
- How many potential buys and at what price targets or percentage change?
- Am I prepared to buy if the stock drops 10 to 20 to 50%? How would you react?
- Would you question your judgment and consider selling if it drops 10 to 20 to 50%?
- What is the projected holding time of the asset?
- At what price points or allocation percentage of total portfolio would you consider taking some off the table?
- If the stock grows to a commanding percentage of your portfolio, how would you respond to rebalance? Would you be prepared to pull the principle or more?

As investors, we need to change the paradigm. Drops are good. It's how you react and if you're proactive with your strategy. I recall the flash crash 2018, markets were getting hammered. A financial advisor messaged me on LinkedIn to help discuss any concerns I had. I was met with silence when replying I was "loving it." And I wasn't referring to my "happy meal." That is why we keep cash on hand to take advantage of such opportunities. In ten years, we will be glad they got slammed.

Some of the largest market crashes are listed below. They all have one commonality in that they were opportunities to build wealth faster. Why? When markets tank, the probability of appreciation rises. If you held strong, and better yet bought through the corrections, it would be unlikely you'd be dependent on wages today. Take a peek:

1907 Panic[8]: -20%
Crash of 1929: -85%
Black Monday (1987): -20%
Dot Com Bubble (2000): -75%
Financial crisis of 2008: - 20%

As I'm writing this, markets are correcting at the fastest rate since the 2008 financial crisis. The culprit; coronavirus. Is it an overreaction? I would never underplay a tragedy where lives are lost and pray its milder than anticipated. But being a novel virus, there is a great degree of uncertainty. This causes people to act sporadically, fearing the market will go to zero. Is that possible? If it did, we'd have much bigger problems. For that to occur, titans like Amazon, Netflix, Google, Apple, etc. would all go out of business. Has anyone watched Netflix or searched Google lately?

When turmoil and uncertainty approach, markets react. We need to anticipate these and keep cash on deck.

---

[8] https://www.businessinsider.com/biggest-stock-market-crashes-in-history

Corrections are the greatest gift to your finances the market will ever wrap you. There will always be someone chanting doomsday, luring the herd to sell. But a temporary correction is a temporary chance to build wealth faster. Short-term fear does not reduce long term worth or growth of businesses. It is a provisional opportunity to capitalize on discounts. The paradigm should change accordingly.

History can lend a guiding hand. The worst novel virus on record was the Spanish Flu. In 1918-20, it infected about 25% of the world's population over a two-year period, accounting for more than 50 million deaths. The impact on the stock market was relatively low. Fortunately, many differences exist today than 100 years ago. We share data faster and have more advanced medical systems. This works in our favor in finding treatments, vaccines, and reducing deaths. It can also help in anticipating the magnitude of market drops.

In the coronavirus case, we can more immediately look to China as it was first to be affected. The Chinese stock market actually rose to two-year highs around 60 days after the first reported cases. This may be useful information in translating to the magnitude of effect on the U.S. stock markets, in addition to how long market turmoil will afford us discounted prices.

Normally, we vigilantly scout out opportunities that have the potential to outperform the market. In times of distress, we move back to the basics. What sound companies participated in discounts? If all were affected similarly, the choices should be easy. When the Coronavirus first started rattling markets, I immediately made a list of the top ten companies I've been waiting to go on sale. Some of the names were Tesla, Wayfair, Nike, Disney, Match group, Facebook, and TJX. These companies had realized major gains over the past few years. Temporary uncertainty didn't make them half as valuable. Rather, it reflected institutional systems firing sell orders to mitigate risk, disrupting supply and demand, and causing investors make emotionally motivated decisions.

The herd of investors doesn't understand the value of long-term. They are impatient and tend to invest with money the need to cover financial obligations, or want to "time" the market and protect against further "losses." But no stock genie knows the direction or magnitude of market moves, aside that markets tend to move upward over time. No money invested should be money you need in the short-term and you'll only lose during downfalls if you sell. Holding strong, and deploying cash reserves is key to obtaining long term returns.

In addition, investing today is largely guided by computer programs. Most financial professionals talk about how the next market "crash" will be due to factors like inflation, deflation, interest rates, etc. The truth is, the long-term impact of these metrics is very low. The actual movement comes from systemic parameters that move large amounts of money into and out of the market, overwhelming the supply and demand equation. Varying risk or market levels force programs to sell in large amounts that further exemplify corrections. This is an opportunity for individual investors to leverage intuition, taking advantage of where computers fall short.

In 2008, many saw their portfolios drop 40-50%. Most reacted by selling. It's not because they were trying to time the market. They didn't anticipate or prepare to hold long term. They panic because their finances are in a state of crisis. They may need the money invested in the near term because they can't afford their lifestyle. If you need a penny from your investment accounts, you will not succeed in markets.

Or they handed their stash to their broker, or other money manager, trusting them to follow the best path. Most get commissions regardless of success, and often are not required to work under the fiduciary standard. Translation: they don't have your best interest in mind. They are making money, just not for you, rather from you. Having many clients, they often take a cookie cutter approach to investing. It's a truly broken industry.

Although your advisor is making commissions (and charging a you fee) off selling processed, pre-packaged products (Oscar Mayer deli-fresh turkey breast anyone?), odds are they have no retirement plan themselves.

But back to corrections. There's another class of bright-eyed individuals with their wallets ready. Let's call them "the uber wealthy." Over the next five to ten years following the 2008 crash, many millionaires were made. And it wasn't only people that just started investing or that just happened to time the bottom. It was those that had a strategy and held their ground. They had cash on hand and went on a shopping spree. The ultimate recovery made the drop but a small bump in the road, or a bridge to freedom for those waiting patiently. The wealthy are not concerned about the next "crash." They don't know when or if it's coming. But they are positioned to thrive whether it arrives or not (more-so if it does). Another point to mention about corrections:

They are often followed by a pseudo-crash, around 12-15 months after the previous bottom. Why is this? Interest rates? Deflation? Inflation? No, No, and No. It's much simpler. If I've learned anything about wealthy entities, it's this. They are patient to wait for opportunities, and when they do, they hate paying taxes on gains. The pseudo-crash occurs simply because big money knows how to retain profits. They scrape up securities during turmoil and wait until the 12-month and 1 day mark to unload some. This strategy cuts their capital gains taxes in half, typically from 40 to 20%. When you are running with big money, it comes out to a massive number.

The current correction is not the first time and won't be the last. And they all have one thing in common. Violent recovery when the clouds clear. All the corrections in history are minuscule in perspective to forward market levels achieved. If you are in this for the long run and play by the right strategies, you should expect and look forward to them. Be prepared to capitalize with cash reserves.

Make a contract with yourself to invest "x%" of your income whether markets rise or fall. When they do fall, contribute even more, and be content knowing that you're paying less than everyone else. Be sure to eat your Wheaties in depressed markets. It's time to channel the courage of your inner Tony the tiger.

Will it take time? Absolutely, and that's a good thing if you're young. More time allotted to build your portfolio at a reasonable price and to allow it to grow. For the old timers, it could be a nightmare if their allocations aren't appropriate. We will explain in a jiffy.

The Players

Before we dig into asset allocation, I want to briefly introduce the players.

When most books talk about asset allocation, they are referring to broad categories like stocks and bonds. Although I include bonds, they have little utility in the building phase of wealth. This is inconsistent with what is taught in most financial texts. They discuss in detail how to retain wealth with bonds, insurance, annuities and the-like, but fail to map the blueprint to obtain it first. A tip to those fellow authors, the majority of your readers are not wealthy yet!

Dissecting stocks further, we discover plenty of variety, that in turn comes with different utility. Warning: the lineup that is most sensible to me may be slightly unconventional to the pundits. But it has worked "for me so back off! (In Billy Madison tone)"

Below you will find a brief description of each, along with their utility, risk equivalent (RE), and reward potential (RP). To my knowledge, these are not standardized measures. I made them up! The scale is measured in 1-10 form, with 1 being low risk and low reward, and 10 being high risk and high reward. We will revisit each in a later chapter to define in greater detail.

- Cash (RE: 1; RP: 0)
  - Parked in reserve fund to deploy under turmoil
  - Although cash in itself does not grow, it can store kinetic energy. When things go south, its magnitude for earning potential is exponential
  - It does carry some risk due to inflation as prices typically go up in the future. We will discuss later its utility in position scaling.
  - Potential of 10% losses or more during inflation turmoil
- Bonds (RE:2; RP2)
  - A company takes a loan from investors and offers to pay them a coupon or "interest" rate
  - Utility to anchor portfolio against risk exposure
  - Potential of 20 percent losses or more during turmoil
- ETFs/Index fund (RE:3; RP: 3)
  - A basket of individual securities or investment vehicles that is essentially a pre-made portfolio
  - Limited risk due to wide security exposure, but inhibited potential returns due to overdiversification and fees
  - Utility to reduce overall and improve ability to acquire additional risk exposure with moderate long term capital appreciation
  - Potential of 30 percent losses or more during turmoil
- Big caps/value stocks (RE:4; RP: 4)
  - Large market capitalization (or company value)
  - Allows introduction of risk exposure of other vehicles
  - Utility in stabilizing portfolio in moderate capital appreciation and/or dividend yields

- Potential of 40 percent losses or more during turmoil
- REITs (RE:5; RP: 5)
  - Real estate investments trusts are companies that own pools of income producing real estate
  - Provide large dividends yields and moderate long term capital appreciation
  - Potential of 50 percent losses or more during turmoil
- Foreign markets (RE: 5; RP 5)
  - Utility to introduce exposure to other economies of scale
  - Utilized to hedge against risk of overexposure to single economic system and to tap into heavy growth trends
  - Potential of 50 percent losses or more during turmoil
- Small caps (RE:6; RP: 6)
  - Small market capitalization, often a product of young market share or earnings capitalization
  - Historically have the capacity to outperform Big caps in attaining moderate-high long term capital appreciation returns in exchange for greater risk exposure
  - Potential of 60 percent losses or more during turmoil
- Growth stocks (RE: 7; RP: 7)
  - Business with historical capital appreciation that is well above average due to rapid earnings growth
  - Utility in high long term capital appreciation in exchange for high volatility

- o Potential of 70 percent losses or more during turmoil
- Initial public offerings (IPOs) (RE: 8; RP: 8)
  - o Private entity that offers ownership to the public to raise capital
  - o High short-, mid-, and long-term capital appreciation potential in exchange for severe volatility
  - o Potential of 80 percent losses or more during turmoil
- New Markets (RE:9; RP: 9)
  - o An entire new segment that is ridden with regulatory and earnings potential uncertainty
  - o High short-, mid-, and long-term capital appreciation potential in exchange for severe volatility
  - o Potential of 90 percent losses or more during turmoil
- Distressed (RE: 9; RP: 9)
  - o A potential bargain, often facing temporary headwinds and uncertainty
  - o Utility in shorter term entry and exit points to capitalize on large swings in share price
  - o Potential of 90 percent losses or more during turmoil
  - o High risk, high potential reward
- Bankrupt (RE:10; RP: 10)
  - o Companies that have filed for chapter 11 bankruptcy protection in attempt to restructure and come out a stronger company
  - o Extreme uncertainty and volatility with the possibility of massive returns if process is successful

- Utilized for short term capitalization of massive movements through the chapter 11 process, or mid-term in hopes restructuring is successful
- Often, original shareholders are wiped out if the process is unsuccessful due to being last in line to creditors for payouts. New stock may be reissued without any recovery for prior shareholders.
- Potential of 100 percent losses during turmoil

Note, I have estimated the potential percentage loss that could be utilized in gauging anticipated volatility and risk. However, this is speaking for the asset class in general. Individual securities can vary widely, and may be further dissected to gauge their risk potential. Each bucket, in itself, should be further diversified.

Below is a tool to quantify your risk exposure (RX). Note, this is not required. But if you are looking to gauge how your general allocations translate to your specific risk tolerance, it can provide some guidance. It can also assist in blueprint construction of your personal portfolio:

Risk exposure (RX) = (% allocation of personal portfolio x Risk equivalent (RE)) + (repeat same calculation (%allocation x RE) for each held allocation/position)

Ex/allocations below represent the % of each "player" or bucket of securities in your total portfolio, multiplied by their respective risk equivalent

Small caps 10% = (0.1x6) = 0.6

Growth stocks: 16% (0.16x7) = 1.12
Big caps/value Stocks: 30%. (0.3x4) = 1.2
New markets 5% (0.05x9) = 0.45
I.P.O.s: 5%. (0.05x8) = 0.4
Distressed assets: 7.5%. (0.075x9) = 0.675
Foreign markets: 4%. (0.04x5) = 0.2
REITS – 4% (0.04x5) 0.2
Bonds: 4%. (0.04x2) = 0.08
Bankrupt: 2% (0.02x10) =0.2
ETFs/index funds: 2.5%. (0.025x3) = 0.075
Cash – 10% (0.1x1) = 0.1

RX = (0.6) + (1.12) + (1.2) + (0.45) + (0.4) + (0.675) + (0.2)
(0.2) + (0.08) + (0.2) + (0.075) + (0.1) = 5.3

Key (1-10 scale)
1 -Ultra low risk, low return potential
5 – Moderate risk, moderate return potential
10 – Ultra high risk, high return potential

Although it's counterintuitive, I've only included a reference point for 1,5, and 10. Your portfolio can fall anywhere in between based on your individual risk tolerance.

As you can see, each listed class has a different utility. Hence, it's allocation in your portfolio should be geared toward your individual risk tolerance. There's no disputing the reality that classes with larger risk profiles have outperformed those of lower risk. The best investors are the best at understanding how to manage risk. They sacrifice the lowest potential loss for the greatest potential rewards. How you map your portfolio becomes a tradeoff between risk and returns. Only you can make the rules. Most resources neglect to provide visibility into how you can utilize risk profiles to build positions in a way that actually enhances returns. We'll discuss how.

Here's the caveat; the players can change. An IPO can transition into a growth stock like any of the players can become distressed. Over time, there's a tendency for the asset classes with higher risk to grow to disproportionately large percentages of your portfolio. This affords us the funding to potentially take on a higher risk tolerance, and greater flexibility in the way we rebalance and allocate our portfolio. We will discuss further later.

Most of our holdings should have a longer-term horizon, taking advantage of volatility along the way. When turmoil arrives, the higher risk equivalents drop faster. But the reverse also proves true as we exit the storm. How we scale into each position plays a major role in managing risk as well as our overall return potential. Next, we will discuss how to utilize the players to map out your portfolio blueprint.

The Blueprints

I'm hoping you are reading this as early as I started investing. If not, it will still benefit you and make a valuable hand me down to younger friends and family members. But age matters in investing.

When you are younger, you have a higher risk tolerance and more time to allow your investments to grow. Compound interest is like adding fuel to the fire. The higher your account balance gets, the more rapidly it grows. You can afford to buy riskier assets, like growth stocks and young companies. When you are older, you don't have those luxuries. As previously hinted, I'm not just talking about bonds versus stocks, but also the individual stock types within your portfolio.

Let's first map out a rough guide of how your portfolio should be allocated based on age, then we will discuss the individual allocations. As the clock ticks forward, you should move from the building to maintaining stage, seeking haven when you can't afford as much risk.

The retirement portion of your portfolio is a bit boring. Yet, it's setting you up for guaranteed comfort for the gold watch ceremony. We should shoot to contribute at least the max employer match for our 401k. Most companies offer up to six percent, which is about the only free lunch you'll ever be served. That means, up to 6% of your salary is essentially doubled by your employer, before accounting for any additional investment returns. AKA you gain 100% principle off the bat! I like those odds. Take full advantage of this. If plausible, you should try to contribute up to the maximum deduction allowable for that tax year to reduce your taxable income. For 2020, the max is $19,500 per individual. It generally rises with time. If you are over 50 and have been playing the wrong hands, all is not lost. You are given a larger "catch up" allotment of $26,000 annually. But the hope of this guide is to set you up, so you don't have the need to work past 50. Preferably much sooner.

Ensure you read your employer prospectus to check on fees. Most are reasonable. But if they aren't, you can research synergistic retirement plan opportunities outside your company to enhance returns. Although this money grows tax-free, you need to tip Uncle Sam a healthy portion, known as income tax, when you start withdrawing after 59 1/2

This is where the I.R.A. account comes into play. Historically, tax rates have been much higher than those we enjoy today, although it doesn't seem that way. Whether that will change in your retirement is like predicting doomsday. But I.R.A. accounts are a great tool to hedge the potential risk of higher taxes.

The traditional I.R.A. account will also allow for some immediate tax advantages for those who qualify. But many with higher incomes will not. The Roth I.R.A. is ideal for high earners, as they can take advantage of paying taxes on contributions now and withdrawing scot-free when retirement comes. In the face of tax turmoil, this will pack a powerful punch in your retirement corner.

Your personal portfolio will be the major determinant in if you become uber wealthy. Note these ranges are initial portfolio mapping suggestions and can change with your personal situation and risk tolerance. Over time, you should transition to the wealth retention stage where you'll hold a greater proportion of low-risk assets.

If you are 50 or older, you should be on the back nine of your retirement planning. Even better, just working on your golf game. Having a high proportion of risky assets after that period can severely damage your nest egg. Start early and be consistent. Investing, it's not a one-time thing, but a lifestyle.

The different portions of your portfolio need to be allocated in a way whereas losing an entire individual investment won't matter. If you have $100k in assets with 2% in chapter 11 companies, and all of them go to zero, you gave yourself multiple shots at a home run in exchange for very low risk.

Total portfolio (retirement + personal accounts + cash). *(All ages)*
0-50% cash reserves/savings.
30-45% retirement accounts.
Personal portfolio: 45-55%.
Retirement portfolio magnified *(All ages)*
I.R.A. account: 30%.
IRA magnified.

- ETFs/Index funds: 60%.
- Bonds: 30%.
- Stocks: 10%.
  401k: 70%.
  o Employer matched and managed funds.

Personal portfolio magnified

Security types: age 0-35.

Small caps10%

Growth stocks: 20%.

Big caps/value Stocks: 30%.

New markets 5%

I.P.O.s: 15%.

Distressed assets: 7.5%.

Foreign markets: 5%.

REITS – 5%

Bonds: 0-5%.

Bankrupt: 0-2%

ETFs/index funds: 2.5%.

0-2% day/swing trading reserve.

Security types (Age 36-55)

Small caps 5%

Growth stocks: 15%.

Big caps/value stocks: 35%.

New markets- 2.5%

I.P.O.s: 10%.

Distressed assets: 5%.

Foreign markets: 5%.

REITS – 7.5%

Bonds: 15%.

E.T.F.s/Index funds: 5%.

0-2% day/swing trading reserve.

Security types (Age 56-grave)
Small caps: 2.5%
Growth stocks: 5%.
Big caps/value stocks: 10%
New markets: 2.5%
I.P.O.s: 2.5%.
Distressed assets: 2.5%.
Foreign markets: 2.5%.
REITS -7.5%
Bonds: 50%.
E.T.F.s/Index funds: 25%.
0-2% day/swing trading reserve.

Note, between each category of assets, there will be some crossover. Try to select the best suited label and roll with it. I like to think of each section as a bucket, and always look back to the allocation percentages when finding new opportunities or building positions to see how it will impact the overall portfolios well-being. In addition to previously discussed strategies, the allocation percentage offer additional risk mitigation. The higher volatile classes tend to grow faster and have greater earnings potential. If they don't, at least initially, the lower risk classes grow at a steady enough rate to make that okay. They are in place to afford us greater risk exposure opportunities that will build measurable wealth. All while getting a good night's rest.

Don't get tied up in trying to make each category exact as markets are constantly changing. The portfolio mapping suggestions are in relation to principal money commitment to your initial blueprints. The structure should initially be more rigid, but the situation is fluid. This should serve as an initial blueprint. Write it down so you have an idea of your allocation goals. As your account grows you may decide to change your risk tolerance, as you'll likely have more "house money" to play with, and make additional judgments with regard to appropriate allocation changes.

In addition to the general allocations, each category should have a balance of different sectors. For example, in the Big caps/value stocks portion, we wouldn't want to buy all retail stocks (i.e. Walmart, Target, CVS, and Kroger). We want to have a variety that works in tandem to weather lagging industries and guarantee stable returns. A few examples include energy, materials, consumer staples, health care, and information technology. We'd also want a solid number of investments in each category to tip the probabilities in our favor. If you have one stock in IPOs, you are asking for trouble. If you have 10, and your right 30% of the time, those 3 securities will likely allow the remaining 7 underperformers to dissipate without any measurable wake. In fact, one or two of them will likely be the name on the stern of your Yacht.

Place Your Bets

There's a strategy in blackjack where you can greatly improve your odds of winning. Start low, go slow, and double your bet after each loss. When you win a hand, restart the process. Although your odds of winning improve, an unlucky streak can clean out your wallet. Unlike blackjack, in investing, there's no cap limits. So is investing like gambling? In some ways. Gambling is not a typical path to building wealth unless you are someone like Phil Helmuth. But learned strategies in investing greatly improve your odds of "winning."

Some studies have shown picking great stocks is like throwing darts at a dartboard. Portfolio performance has been replicated by complete randomness. But research, strategy, and intuition can give us a leg up.

Like gambling, you can invest more initially if you know you have a good chance of winning. I recall as a younger adult; friends and I would bring our paychecks from the local grocer up to the casino. We'd walk in and be fast approached by the money wheel.

Playing the money wheel requires little skill. You can place your bet to guess which numbers will be selected on a spin. The odds of rolling $1 are high, as they occupy 24 out of 54 slots. Landing on one will pay a multiple of one.

The odds of rolling a joker are much lower, occupying 1 out of 54 slots, but pays a multiple of 40.

Would you feel more comfortable betting your hard-earned money on $1 or Joker? Like me, probably $1. But the joker still has an important utility. If we bet smaller amounts on joker in conjunction with low-risk bets, we can still earn at a high probability while simultaneously leaving the door open for bigger gains. All while keeping our shirt.

It's not a perfect analogy and works in our favor to a greater degree when building an elite portfolio. Point being, investing does involve playing the probabilities to ensure success. We want to aim for having both high and low risk stocks in our portfolio. To mitigate risk, the bulk of our portfolio will be the tried and true big caps and value stocks that allow us to sleep well at night. But we don't want to leave the small caps, I.P.O.s, and growth stocks completely off the table. These will be the X factors that allow us to build measurable wealth quickly when approached responsibly. Again, their names will be the ones that wind up as decals on your yacht's caboose.

There's a relevant financial theory that begs to be mentioned here. It's called prospect theory. It suggests, investors typically fear losses more than they value gains. Meaning, the emotional magnitude of losing trumps the elation of winning. As a result, most tend to neglect high risk securities in exchange for being comfortable. As a result, most fail to build measurable wealth.

A financial advisor, let's call him Scott, recently called me out. He said, I only report my gains. Although I do enjoy discussing them more, here is why the losers don't matter. Successfully playing the probabilities.

Let's look at an example looking directly at face value gains vs. losses. This reflects an actual snapshot in time at one point of some of my biggest gainers and losers. If you owned 10 stocks of equal weight, with $1 of principle in value each for simplicity, and have the following results:

1) +1500%
2) +500%
3) +400%
4) +200%
5) +100%
6) 0
7) -15%
8) -30%
9) -35%
10) -100%

That would reflect a total gain of over +250%. And it simply demonstrates utility of probabilities, without inclusion of any strategies we've discussed thus far. It brings to light an important school of thought that prevents most from building wealth. Fear. Losses are fixed. Gains are limitless. I want to present another point here. Most financial "experts" harp on using stop losses as a strategy to manage risk. If this sounds like your money manager, don't walk, RUN! There are superior ways to manage risk. The above gains represent some actually positions in my portfolio. Had I set a stop loss, at say 50% in the red, positions 1 through 5 would have afforded me a realized loss.

Stop losses do offer perceived value preservation, but often at the cost of upside potential. It speaks to another mindset that prevents most from building wealth. The stimulus that defers from the desired result is more likely to be remembered. I.e. the emotional magnitude of losses outweighs that of equivalent gains. The result is a tendency to shift focus to "not losing" rather than outcomes. This can be costly. There is a much better way.

In fact, share price depreciation should be a part of your strategy to yield massive gains that outweigh any losers. Even with results like position 10 above. Ahead, we will learn additional strategies to build an elite portfolio that welcomes and even craves volatility. It will serve us kindly in the long run.

We're also buying stocks of varying nature and utilizing strategies at a higher degree with risky equities. We know that higher risk assets are more volatile, so we want to start lower and go slower along our sliding scale. These tend to sink like an anchor when things are rocky and launch into space when the dust settles. Think of stocks like SNAP, HEXO, and Pinterest. For our big players that are less volatile, we are investing more initially to prevent missing out on gains and to stabilize the riskier portions of our portfolio. These are the Proctor & Gambles, United Healthcare, John Deer's, etc. I don't foresee the majority of folks skipping toilet paper, health insurance, or cutting the grass anytime soon. But the allocations matter. Having a higher proportion of less risky assets allows us to introduce the risk that welcomes massive returns.

Follow the Leader

There's an analogy in leadership that is applicable to investing. Leaders of all levels have many competing priorities. It's a challenge to complete all of them. So how can they prioritize effectively to ensure the most important tasks get completed?

If we take a painter's bucket with limited space allocation, but want to fill it with rocks, sediments, and other materials varying size and shape, how can we get the most bang for our buck? We have our big rocks or most important priorities. Then smaller rocks and particles, all the way down to grains of sand and water—the potentially urgent but unimportant priorities. If we want to ensure execution of the most important tasks, we need to put the big rocks first. Followed by smaller rocks, sand, water, and so forth. If we try to enter the small items first, we will run out of room for the bigger, more important tasks.

With investing, there are many stocks worthy of occupying your portfolio. You need to determine the key components you want to prioritize first. The sure things and heavy hitters. If you start with adding speculative or unknowns to the pile initially, you'll run out of room in your bucket for the most impactful positions. Take advice from fools, and you will become one.

At the same time, we are not just trying to crown a couple of princesses. We need our portfolio to work together as a team. If one position is lagging, the others need to pick up the slack, so the flywheel continues turning in the right direction.

Within the example below, let's further demonstrate fund allocations to different sectors. Inside of my 30% big caps and 10% small caps *(age 0-35)*, I would select a diverse array of securities and estimate the goal percentage allotment for each security making up that basket. For example, if I wanted to build positions in five stocks per section, I would plan to prioritize my most important stocks accordingly.

Big caps magnified: 30% of total personal portfolio.
United Healthcare: 25%.
John Deer: 25%.
General Electric: 20%.
Apple: 15%.
AbbVie pharmaceuticals: 15%.

Small caps magnified: 10% of personal portfolio.
Snap: 20%.
Groupon: 25%.
Pinterest: 20%.
Square: 20%.
Beyond Meat: 15%.

As time goes on and resources allow, you can start adding new positions and reallocate goal percentages. Keep in mind; this will be an estimated blueprint that we work toward over time, as we are not purchasing the stocks in full amounts initially. We may decide to shoot for this disbursement over a period of six to twelve months or longer. But we'd foresee less volatility with big caps, meaning closer targets where we will pull the trigger, and potentially fewer total buys to get to our initial target position faster. An example to illustrate the difference would look like this:

United Healthcare Purchase Plan
Initial share price target: $100.
Buy 1: 25 shares @$100.
Buy 2 target: 50 shares @$95.
Buy 3 target: 75 shares @ $90.
Buy 4 target: 100 shares @ $85.

Note here that we have four buys accounting for a potential variance of around 15% total, and the first is a relatively sizable position. In this manner, we are reducing our chances of leaving gains off the table. We can rightfully assume that ten years from now, emergency rooms will still have long wait times on Christmas Eve (or any day for that matter) with one doctor working.

With a small cap or IPO stock that hasn't found the formula for sustainable profitability yet, we'd want to tread more carefully. This would result in a larger variance for targets and a greater number of planned buys to mitigate risk. Where with United Healthcare we planned for a potential drop of 15%, here, we account for a potential downfall of over 60%. Also, our final purchase is about equivalent in monetary value to our initial purchase of the more stable company. We will further quantify the potential risk of individual securities in the next chapter, to give you a better idea of how to set specific targets.

Groupon Purchase Plan
Initial share price: $5.
Buy 1: 50 shares @$5.
Buy 2: 100 shares @4.50.
Buy 3: 200 shares $ 3.99.
Buy 4: 400 shares at $3.50.
Buy 5: 600 shares at $2.99.
Buy 6: 800 shares @$2.50.
Buy 7: 1000 shares @ $1.99.
Buy 8: 1300 shares @$1.50.

With the higher risk small cap above, we are reducing our risk in a few ways. The first is the total value and position percentage in our portfolio is lower. The second is we plan on doubling the number of total buys in smaller blocks, as we know small caps are notoriously more volatile. The third is we are planning for a bigger potential total drop. In this strategy, we are hopeful that the stock drops, so we can build a robust position at a good value. As the stock loses ground, we'll keep buying as planned. If it rises, we will let it ride or have the option to transition to a Dollar-cost averaging strategy. If we foresee new scenarios where the outlook is poor, we can change course or cut some losses in a tax efficient manner. In this regard, we'll rest easily knowing we didn't jump the gun too quickly by following our risk mitigation strategy.

This is a real-life example. One of my top allotments for small caps in my portfolio was Groupon. It scored well in my stock picking "formula" that lies ahead. I bought the stock and watched it rise from $2.92 up to $6.50. Originally angered that the stock rose so fast, fear set in when it started reverting before taking any profit. So, should I have sold it at $6.50? If given a mulligan, I would have taken a percentage out, up to the principal amount invested.

Not making the best-selling plays. I learned from Groupon. But my position was small. It was a rarity where I caught the bottom within the first two buys, and it rose from there, disallowing much depth into the scheduled buy targets. But I was able to transition to dollar cost averaging to continue building out that position. As a side note, you won't always, and don't need to get all the way through your buy targets. We are utilizing a scale to ensure we aren't exposing ourselves to overt risk. If you are dead wrong, it will save you from catastrophic damage. We'll be wrong sometimes and things won't pan out perfectly. In investing in stocks, there will be many short bursts of adrenaline like this. If you follow the strategies, you can turn them into moments of peace. Move on with wisdom and continue to set goals affording high probabilities of gains while limiting risk. Don't get greedy when an opportunity arises to sell some and play with the "houses money."

Moving forward, Groupon stock is making new lows with a recent one day drop of over 40%. Being one of my top picks in my small cap bucket, I was caught off guard.

But, also, curious and excited. What had happened? The stock had announced poor fourth quarter holiday results, disassembling of its low margin goods business, and a possible reverse stock split of 10-1. I had to break these apart, piece by piece, to determine my next steps. I had followed my risk mitigation strategy of buying slowly along my scale, but this drop was outside of the expected range.

Could there be a world without Groupon's 50 million users? Possibly, but that massive user base could also summon opportunity. Google had offered the company a $6 billion buyout bid a few years back that was rejected, and the recent drops value the company at under $450 million. Was what they announced really that bad? Shattering a failing portion of their business and focusing on the profitable side? A potential $1 trillion market for daily deals.

Big companies acquire smaller ones in a space of interest for several reasons. One is, it's easier to build out an existing business than laying a new foundation. It generally starts with some "expert" analysts screaming overvalued. And by traditional standards, they are often correct. But it isn't just about the balance sheet. Big companies are willing to pay top dollars for a user base primed to monetize. One previous example was YouTube. In 2006 it was purchased by google. Many experts and even shareholders felt they overpaid at a valuation of $1.65 billion. But Google didn't see a balance sheet. They saw potential in the userbase and had the leadership and resources to make it happen, all while diversifying their company. YouTube is estimated to be worth over $170 billion today.

I was still a believer in Groupon and marked it off as an opportunity. Scraping up shares that the market had undervalued after emotionally reacting to headlines, I was confident when the clouds cleared, bright skies would emerge. Moving forward a year, I was sitting on a 650% long-term gain. This time, I didn't miss the opportunity to take some off the table and didn't allow my *contributed* allotment (or principal) exceed the originally intended allocation percentage. If I was wrong, it wouldn't have made a measurable dent in the performance of my overall portfolio.

My perception was Groupon's fate was likely a buyout or healthy turnaround, rather than bankruptcy. During a bad quarter, it pushes out $650 million in sales. A sub $450 million valuation would have someone knocking.

When major falls occur in securities you own, you need to change the paradigm. If you didn't own the stock, and the same 40% drop occurred, would you be intrigued to start a new position? If you didn't know the share price, and couldn't access it, would you still be an owner? If the answer for these questions is definitely not, it may be time to sell. If it's possibly or heck, yes, you need to act quickly. How does having an invested position change your perspective versus being a bystander? Could Groupon close shop and leave its massive user base hanging? Is any new talent on deck to improve operations? Any mergers or buyers better geared to turn the business model around? If so, what's a reasonable price? These are the types of questions you should be asking. In a situation like Sears or JC Penny, my answers would be grimmer.

Websites and applications with large user bases are a different animal. The struggle and fight to gain online user traffic is real. Like a physical store merchandising goods to lure extra sales as you walk through, websites are no different.

Now let's talk about what makes stocks tick and how to identify value that will shatter expected returns.

Great Investors Ask Great Questions

I repeat: If you didn't know the share price, would you still buy the stock?

So what makes a stock move and how can I pick the right ones?

You'll find many tricks of the trade in financial texts. But what I'm about to share is my personal formula for picking stocks. It's simple, yet effective in determining potential vehicles to park your money. This method allows you to quantify potential value and risk by zeroing in on the most important variables that make stocks to move.

We'll create a scale to compare different assets. Each variable is assigned a value in parentheses, indicating its estimated impact or importance. The number inside represents the maximum value each stock could be assigned for that category, based on potential impact. Insert the security being researched for each point and tally up the total. Then compare it to the key, which reflects a scale of very low to very high risk.

If a stock doesn't score well, it doesn't necessarily mean it should be neglected. Low scoring securities can make massive moves in either direction. As an example, Tesla scored a 62 when I started purchasing it years ago. It is better suited as a measure of risk and has most utility in determining the weight of each security in the concurrent asset class. We'd want to follow more copious risk mitigation strategies for lower scoring assets and anticipate them being a smaller proportion of our portfolio with a well-planned purchasing strategy. Without further ado:

(10) General chart pattern/timing.

- What is the general trajectory of the chart? Does it have any history of violent cycles? Where does it stand in the current cycle? Does it radiate volatility? Based on these factors, how do you feel purchasing the stock during this snapshot it time?

(8) 52-week range

- Where does the stock stand in its 52-week range? How far below or above that range could you foresee it dropping/rising based on known or projected information? How about based on the type of asset class it falls in?

- For most stocks, we'll want to buy more toward the bottom of the range. Especially for value stocks that have slow growth and a history of predictable fluctuations.

- Exceptions may include high growth stocks, highly anticipated I.P.O.s, or circumstances that we can easily foresee the upward momentum continue.

(5) PE Ratio

- The price to earnings ratio = earnings per share x the share price. Essentially, it is a measure of perceived value. High means "expensive" and low means "cheap." But it's current value often represents the potential for earnings growth, so is best used as a comparison tool. Is the price to earnings ratio reasonable? How does it compare to its own industry? The general market? Do earnings and future projections validate the PE ratio?

- Does it appear the stock is on sale or overpriced?
- Note: you need to have an eclectic understanding here. Although P/E ratios have utility, in themselves they should not be the driving force of your decisions. Low and high P/E values don't always mean "cheap" and "expensive" respectively. There is more to the story. (Hence, why the potential magnitude of effect accounts for 5 of 118 possible points)

(10) General feeling/prospects

- What is your perception of the future of the company? Is it guaranteed to be around in five to ten years?
- What opportunities do they have for expansion of market share or new industry penetration? Are they expanding the parameters of their business?
- Do a lot of people use the services/products? Is the customer base growing or shrinking?

(10) Earnings/revenue growth potential

- What are the future earnings and revenue projections? Do they seem feasible? Do they have a history of meeting or exceeding projections?
- Does the company have clear opportunities for growth?

- If not yet profitable, are sales or userbase growing? Are losses shrinking?

(8) Management/leadership

- Shareholders are the owners of the company and want to know two things; the size and consistency of dividends and market value of their shares. They want to know how the CEO/board will achieve profitable growth. Do executives have a history of meeting shareholder and employee expectations? What types of accomplishments are they known for?

- Who's the CEO? Are they a visionary leader? What have they accomplished? What motivates them? What does the company culture look like? What are employees saying?

- How are they motivated to ensure success at all levels of business? Are they innovating? Do they have full spectrum of authority in delivering on initiatives and innovations (many big caps CEOs have narrow scope of authority due to bureaucracy)? What are their barriers? How are they controlling expenses or balancing utilizing of resources to grow the business? Are they capitalizing on available opportunities?

(10) Moat/durable competitive advantage.

- Does the company have any competition? If so, does their balance sheet allow them to acquire threats and further enhance market share? What clear competitive advantages do they have over other players? Is the business further scalable? Are their products or services easily replicable?

- What are the barriers to entry in their industry? Were they first to market? Are they leaders in their industry? Is it a novel industry or potential replacement for an existing industry? What would it take to compete?

(8) Buyout potential.

- Have there been bids for the company or similar companies in the past? Do they offer a product or service that could create synergy for other businesses?
- Do they have a large following or user base begging to be monetized?
- Could you foresee them going under without a bailout bid from a bigger company or the government?
- What would be a fair estimation of the company's worth in a buyout? Who are the potential bidders?

(8) Profit/operating margins.

- Is there a healthy bottom line? What do operating margins look like? Are margins growing?
- Is there a history of stable margins?
- Generally, 20+% operating margins here would be an 8/8; 10%:4/8; 5%:2/8, etc. However, be mindful of the industry in question and compare the company to its peers. For example, retail companies have notoriously low margins. You would adjust the scale as you see fit to be more forgiving there.

(5) Consensus.

- What do analysts say about the stock?

- What do analyst research reports say about the company? What are the bull and bear arguments? Are the majority bullish or bearish? What's your analysis?

(5) Analyst price target/fair value estimate

- What's the consensus for the fair value of the stock vs. the current price? Is it undervalued or overvalued based on the available information?

(10) Dividend (5% or higher=10/10; 2.5% = 5/10; 0% = 0/10, etc.)

- Does the stock pay a dividend? At what yield? Is there a history of consistent dividend growth? Any history of dividend cuts or financial strains that could result in cuts in the near future? Is the company rewarding its shareholders?

(5) Insiders holding.

- What percentage of insiders are holding the stock?
- More insiders holding mean those with the most knowledge about the stock, executives, and management have high confidence about future earnings and growth. The higher, the better.

(6) Market cap size (company worth)

- Here, we are trying to capture the forward capital gain potential.
- Historically, small caps and growth stocks outperform big cap and value stocks. We have broken them apart here into four crossover categories in attempt to quantify the forward potential.
- Growth companies add three.

- Value companies add one.
- Small caps add three.
- Large caps add one.
- Example: Google = Growth + Large cap:3+1=4
- Example: Groupon = Growth + Small cap:3+3 = 6
- Example: AMC entertainment holdings = Value + small cap = 1+3=4

(8) Social media "likes"/# of users/application downloads.

- How many likes/followers do they have on social media (Instagram, Facebook, Snap, Twitter, TikTok, etc.)?
- What does the user base look like? Is it growing?
- Is it a popular application? What are people saying about the product/services being offered?
- Is it a disruptor or part of a generational transition? I.e. are younger generations replacing something older generations are using?

(10) Bonus

- Can it make you rich? Or is it a disruptor to an existing industry?
- Could you foresee the stock ticker as the name engraved on the back of your yacht?

The scale isn't by any means perfect. It attempts to quantify the most important metrics that cause stock price movement. You can use it as a tool to research potential value, assess risk, and make educated judgements on quality investments.

Tally up the total and reference the key below to determine if it's a right fit in your portfolio and in what proportion. If it's clearly a winner, you'd want to allocate a greater proportion to those securities in the respective sectors. If it's a lower number, but you still foresee a lot of potential, we'd be more risk averse in its inclusion.

> - <=50 = Very High risk (sell or buy cautiously).
> - 51-69 = High Risk.
> - 70-85 = Moderate Risk.
> - 86-100 = Low Risk.
> - >100 = Very Low Risk (strong buy).
> - Maximum = 118.

Again, a lower total value doesn't mean it has no place in your portfolio. But we'd more carefully consider the ratio and plan out a robust purchasing strategy. The 52-week range can come in handy in estimating potential fluctuations. You'll need to make a further risk assessment to determine how far outside of that range is possible. For a big cap like Nike, it may be safe to assume ten to twenty percent below the 52-week is plausible low if things head south. For a new market small cap like HEXO (marijuana industry), great uncertainty may make 50-99% below fair game. But more than 500% on the upside wouldn't be out of the question either.

For that reason, we'd be more aggressive initially with Nike and start very low and go very slow with HEXO (in relation to the percentage of our portfolio and subsequent buying strategy to accumulate our position).

Another helpful tool is brainstorming industries of the future. Keeping an open ear here is critical. What are the next gens talking about? Where are they spending their time and money? What type of trends are you witnessing? Where are things heading? What is the general direction of high impact industries? Who are the disruptors?

Think about things that will SHOCK our grandchildren. Some of the current ones might include:

1. We filled our cars with gasoline
2. Taxis were driven by people
3. We had "band aid style" healthcare
4. We waited on a list for organs from other people
5. Marijuana was illegal
6. Laypeople had never been to the moon or space
7. We didn't have AI inspired personal assistants
8. People delivered our packages
9. We paid with cash
10. We grew our crops on a farm

What companies do you think will be on the forefront of these changes? Now, consider investing in them!

A good example would be the auto industry. The general trend of the overall industry is from gas combustion engines to electric vehicles (EVs). This presents an opportunity to build market share into an existing industry. Finding trends of this nature, and identifying the disruptors, can heed large returns for shareholders.

At the time of this writing, there are many new exciting markets emerging. There are also markets that we rely on for survival, that we can utilize to anchor our portfolio.

These are important things to ponder when selecting stocks worthy of inclusion. Just a few to consider may be:

- Electric vehicles/batteries.
- Autonomous vehicles.
- Medical marijuana.
- Medical devices.
- 5G connectivity.
- Online shopping and shipping services.
- Solar/alternate energy.
- 3D printing.
- Social media.
- Specialty medications and vaccines.
- Gene therapy.
- Streaming services.
- Health insurance.
- Clean water.
- Genetic food engineering.
- Plant based food.

Great investors ask great questions. In addition to the plethora above, a self-survey can help prioritize your thoughts about specific securities and help contribute to decisions around the percentage of exposure each stock holds in your portfolio. It can also help you decide how many stocks you are comfortable owning.

Here's some additional questions.

How much time do I have weekly to keep up with stock information and research and how many stocks should I own? Based on this, how should I prioritize my big rocks first?

If I could only own five stocks, which would they be? If ten? Fifteen? Twenty?

What class of assets would each fall into? What is my estimated target exposure level? What is the utility of the asset in question and anticipated time horizon of each? Would I consider owning them without knowing the share price?

You can really test your picks by asking yourself the questions below. If you don't like the answers, you may consider reassessing your picks.

If any of the stocks in question dropped more than 50%, how would you feel emotionally, and what would be your respective response?

Which of the above stocks would you admit you were wrong if they turned sour? Based on their respective risk exposure, how will you build out each position to mitigate risk while leaving the table open for gains? What is your individual risk tolerance? When would you consider pulling some principal or beyond off the table? What percentage will you remove and how does it impact the overall blueprint and diversity of your portfolio?

Next, we will build out a portfolio map, and discuss how to position scale into securities based on their risk equivalent.

Money Scrimmage

Like a surgeon prepping to operate, we need to have a well mapped out plan.

Let's use my demographic as an example. I am 33 years old and earn a reasonable salary, too high to contribute to a traditional I.R.A. I potentially have about 32 working years left but want to afford myself the opportunity to retire wealthy earlier. For that reason, I'm going to be a bit riskier than normal, but still set myself up for guaranteed future wealth. I will split my accounts into retirement (35% of total), personal (45% of total), and fluid cash reserves (20%).

I want the majority of my retirement portfolio to be in a tax-deductible account like a 401k. Since my salary is too high to reap the benefits of a traditional I.R.A., a Roth would be most appropriate for the remainder. Remember, we can't predict what future tax rates will be, so a Roth will serve a strategic advantage as it is already taxed at the current rate. Distributions at retirement age will be tax-free, whereas 401k will grow tax-free, but Uncle Sam will be "tipped out" upon disbursements.

I won't pick specific investments here for my retirement accounts. To reduce risk and all but guarantee steady growth, it will contain a higher percentage of E.T.F.s and bonds and less individual stocks.

Cash Reserves
20%

Retirement magnified (35%)
401k: 80% employer managed funds.

Roth I.R.A.: 20% (Bonds: 35%; E.T.F's: 60%; individual stocks: 5%).

Personal magnified (45%)
Big caps: 25%.

Small caps: 10%.

Distressed Assets: 10%.

New markets: 5%

IPOs: 15%.

Growth: 20%.

ETFs: 2.5%

Bankrupt:1%

REITS: 5%

Foreign: 5%

Bonds: 1.5%

Stocks within personal

Big caps
Disney: 15%.

Nike: 12.5%.

United Healthcare: 17.5%.

Starbucks: 10%.

P&G: 10%.

Apple: 17.5%.

Oracle: 10%.

Cisco: 7.5%.

Small caps

Zebra tech. corp.:20%.

ETSY: 15%.

Goodyear: 20%.

Stratasys Limited: 10%.

Hubspot INC.: 15%.

Beyond Meat: 15%.

Groupon: 5%.

Distressed

Teva: 25%.

Kraft-Heinz: 20%.

GE: 20%.

Six Flags: 15%.

AbbVie: 20%.

New markets

HEXO: 20%.

Canopy Growth: 20%.

Arora: 20%.

Cronos: 20%.

Tilray: 20%.

I.P.O's

Pinterest: 20%
UBER: 20%
Crowdstrike: 15%
SmileDirect: 15%
Chewy:15%
Splunk:15%

Growth
Netflix: 12.5%.
Facebook: 15%.
Match Group: 12.5%.
Tesla: 20%.
Square: 15%.
Snap: 10%.
Zillow: 15%

ETFs
Vanguard Small-Cap ETF: 20%
Amplify transformational data sharing ETF: 20%
SPDR S&P China ETF: 20%
iShares Core S&P 500 ETF: 20%
Health Care Select Sector SPDR fund: 20%

Bankrupt
Hertz: 50%
Luckin Coffee: 30%
GNC:10%
Diamond Offshore Drilling: 10%

REITs

Tanger Factory Outlets:15%
Simon Property Group: 15%
Empire State Realty Trust: 15%
Vornado Realty Trust: 15%
American Tower Corp: 25%
Digital Realty Trust: 15%

Foreign

Infosys limited – 15%
Alibaba – 20%
JD.com – 20%
Meituan -15%
ICIC Bank – 10%
Tenecent -20%

Bonds

Vanguard Long-Term Bond ETF – 50%
iShare Core U.S. Aggregate Bond ETF – 50%

So, we built an outline of our portfolio. Does that mean we invest all our allocated savings immediately into the above allotment amounts? Rookie mistake. This is where our buying strategy comes to life. For the less risky sections of our portfolio, the answer may be closer to yes. We need to determine the risk potential of individual securities and set our respective buy targets and time frames.

For a big cap like Disney, we'd want to allocate a bigger portion initially. We'd also plan fewer total purchases to get to our initial goal position and select a shorter time frame range to get to our *initial* allocation (we'd likely continue contributing to this position over the years and readjust our blueprints periodically). We can consider implementing a strategy like dollar-cost averaging if our purchase plan isn't panning out in a reasonable time frame.

Not everyone will have a sizable savings to start with, and that's okay. A lot of our investments will not be from a cash surplus laying around, but income scheduled contributions. The strategies remain the same. Starting with just a few stocks is enough. Companies like Stash make it easy to invest pennies at a time. You can still set buy targets or automate prorated contributions over a selected time frame of your choosing.

If we set a goal to have a total personal portfolio of $100,000 invested over 12 months, and decided on a target allocation of 40% into big caps, that would equate to an initial target allocation of $40,000. Let's say we want 15% of that to be Disney. That would equate to an initial target of $6,085 to fill that position. We would likely select a smaller time block, between 3-6 months, as it represents a lower risk security. With a higher risk security like an IPO, we'd want to extend the time block to take advantage of higher volatility.

Regardless of whether initial contributions come from savings or income, we want to get to our goal position quicker as it's a lower risk security with great growth potential. Disney would be considered a Big cap with a risk equivalent of 4 (see "the players" section). That means, if turmoil arrives, we could account for potential share depreciation of 40 percent or more. The actual percentage you select for your bottom target depends on your individual risk tolerance and time horizon. It could be zero, forty, anywhere in between, or even a dollar-cost averaging strategy that ignores the share price. I would be a little more aggressive here, as Disney could be considered a well-diversified entity, having the luxury of multiple revenue streams. Some with rapid growth, like their streaming business. If we picked a potential volatility scale of 15%, and the share price is currently sitting at $115, our potential bottom would be around $100. The respective buying strategy may look something like this:

Buy target 1: 7 shares @ $115.
Buy target 2: 12 shares @ $110.
Buy target 3: 18 shares @ $105.
Buy target 4: 23 shares @ $100.

The estimated allocation percentages are the initial blueprints for the principal amount invested into our portfolio. It's an unnecessary challenge to try to obtain allotments in the exact planned percentage as markets are extremely fluid. Use your plan as a rough guide. It is helping us get into the game and strategize how we can do so most effectively while limiting risks. We will continually reassess overtime and make any necessary adjustments.

It's also important to note, getting to the target allocation is not the end goal. We would continue purchasing our selected securities over time in appropriate proportions. Unless the utility of the vehicle has expired or we foresee circumstances where the outlook becomes poor. Let's discus the investment vehicles in more detail.

Concentrated Diversity

We pointed to diversity a lot so far. Let's discuss in detail what we mean by that. When you go grocery shopping, you have a list of items needed to stock your kitchen. Or maybe you just buy all hot dogs? With investing, we want to have a variety of different sectors, risk levels, and stock types in our portfolio. We had introduced some different security types previously, that we will now discuss in further detail. Some included growth, IPOs, value, dividend, small caps, big caps, REITS, E.T.F.s, and bonds. You should also consider the diversity of each individual security you own. Do they have multiple streams of revenue?

If you want to build powerful biceps, can you just work out once and expect outcomes? Can you lose that "more to love" status on tinder by eating just one healthy meal? Of course not. It's the consistent daily habits that impact muscle growth and healthy weight management. In addition, you can't pick and choose diet or exercise. Both are required to achieve desired fitness goals. If you work out 7 days a week, but eat an entire gallon of ice cream after each workout, you likely inhibit your intended results.

Investing is the same. There needs to be consistent habits and effort over time to impact portfolio development and realize results. You can't just invest sometimes, or invest, but spend more than you earn on a lifestyle. That will inhibit your net worth potential.

So, you made your plan to work out five days a week. Do you work on the same muscle group every day to get built? Biceps anyone? Like you'd perform an array of exercises for different body parts, you want to hold a variety of stocks that build your portfolio muscles in tandem. Buying a variety of stocks consistently at different prices over time is key.

So how many stocks should you own? Like dating an ex-girlfriend, it's complicated. There isn't a specific size that is one size fits all. But a minimum of five is a sufficient start if allocated properly. If you get into much more than 50, you may be over diversifying. Although diversification is a strategy to mitigate risk, too much can inhibit your returns. Some concentration is necessary to trounce the market average. The goal is to diversify enough to thrive without neglecting the concentration necessary to annihilate the market.

It's much easier to track securities nowadays with the internet. Keep in mind, the more you own, the more time you allot to doing homework. Intuition is still the name of the game, but you should plan to spend at least ten minutes per week, per security, to keep up to date. For a portfolio of 30 securities, that's around five minimum weekly hours to commit to.

Starting with a few key positions and slowly adding more is a good strategy for most beginners. Monitor many companies you know and understand and dip slowly into securities of interest and opportunities that arise. Let's discuss some of the different types of securities you should have in your portfolio to diversify.

Dividend stocks have usually been around for a while, hence often fall into the big cap category, but can encompass any investment vehicle. They offer us an all but guaranteed paycheck either monthly, quarterly, or annually, based on an amount set by the company. It is notated as a dollar amount paid per share owned. As the stock price changes, the percentage of dividend paid changes accordingly (ex/ stock drops, dividend percentage rises). Many strong companies will have consistent dividend increases. There's nothing quite like the gift of cash! A few companies that pay larger dividends are Lowes, Clorox, and Colgate-Palmolive.

Value stocks are also generally big cap companies with solid fundamentals. They are considered to be "on sale" in their respective sectors. One way to determine this is to compare the security in questions price to earnings ratio with that of its peers. If it's much lower, you may consider it a potential value, but there's more to the story. Sometimes it reflects disappointing earnings potential. In many cases, they will also pay a high yield dividend. These companies are utilized for long-term holding periods, offering moderate but stable growth. They can help to anchor your portfolio against higher risk asset classes. Some examples include JP Morgan, Johnson & Johnson, and Berkshire Hathaway.

Growth stocks are sectors or securities that are blessed with rapidly expanding bottom lines, like the tech sector. They can be small or big cap companies. Although they often don't pay a dividend, we tend to be rewarded by faster share price appreciation; related to rapid earnings growth. They often have a high price to earnings ratios compared to the broader market. Although they can appreciate quickly, they also come with higher risk. Warren Buffet tends to neglect growth stocks and the tech industry as he claims to not understand them. If you don't know who that is, Google him. He is wealthy. But not understanding something doesn't mean we have to ignore it. We need tread more carefully and have a strategy in place to mitigate our risk. Although they carry more risk, they tend to heed very large returns for long term investors. Think of companies like Tesla, Amazon, and Apple.

Small caps are companies valued at less than $2 billion. They are generally (but not always) younger, sometimes lesser known companies that can be disruptors in their industry. Based on history, they tend to outperform larger companies over time. Some include Redfin and Groupon. In contrast, large cap stocks are well-known companies that are industry leaders. Resources will define them differently, but often are valued over $5 billion. Examples here include Visa, Microsoft, and Nestle.

Real Estate Investment Trusts (REITs) are facilities that produce income. They include things like apartments, skyscrapers, malls and much more. REITs function similar to a stock. They are sold on public markets in the same manner as individual securities. A big suction for investors is the dividend yields they pay. Although share appreciation is often slower, it is offset by these large dividend payments. It also offers a way to diversify your portfolio without taking on a large financial obligation, like a rental property. No plunger necessary! Some examples include American

Tower Corp., Tanger Factory Outlets, and Simon Property Group.

Initial public offerings (I.P.O.s) are new to the public market. They occur when a private company decides to go mainstream. This marks the first period where anyone can buy newly issued shares. They usually have a high degree of volatility for a variety of reasons. But they can be great opportunities. Buying early into companies like Amazon or Tesla at the initial I.P.O. price has made many individual investors extremely wealthy. Current examples include UBER, AirBNB, and Doordash.

Not all I.P.O's find a quick path to sustainable profitability or share appreciation. Some never do. For that reason, their allotments should encompass a smaller portion of your portfolio, in addition to adhering to stringent purchasing strategies that welcome turmoil. Another important note on IPOs is lock-up periods. Many insiders already own shares prior to the initial public offering date. This is usually very good for them, and has the potential to be bad for you. The first 90 to 180 days of an IPO trading on the market tend to be the most volatile. This is in part a result of lock up periods expiring. Insiders sell at a large profit, causing a large supply of stock that is rarely met with equal demand. For this reason, we should consider an I.P.O. to be exactly that for the first 12 months of trading. Following that period, we can transition it into a more appropriate bucket (i.e. growth).

For the next set of asset classes, I have dedicated entire chapters to illustrate the different utility offered by each. For the aforementioned, we are typically retaining a buy and hold strategy with a longer time horizon.

Distressed Assets

Distressed stocks are companies that are past their glory days or going through a midlife crisis. Some reasons their stocks become depressed are disappointing earnings reports, temporary headwinds, unpopularity, excessive debts, loss of market share, and slowing sales. Some may even be going through bankruptcy. Many continue their doomed descent into darkness, while others find the path forward to resurgence. The goal for investors is to filter out the bent from the broken. These securities contain a high degree of uncertainty and risk but playing the turnaround can reap massive rewards.

Following many stocks is essential to forage opportunities. In today's markets, instantaneous news can send securities on a roller coaster ride. Six Flags, anyone? Much of the time, it's overplayed. Owning shares of struggling companies, or those near bankruptcy can be a huge risk. Yet, what the market may have underpriced can be an opportunity to build positions that heed extraordinary returns. I'll illustrate an example below.

Snapchat is a social media titan in the eyes of new generations. Like we grew up with Facebook, our kids and grandchildren have Snap and Instagram (a subsidiary of

Facebook). The company had its initial public offering for $17 in 2017. It was initially one of the hottest I.P.O's of the year. Moving forward, the company faced some major headwinds. Poor financials and a dwindling user base were the culprits. At one point in 2018, an unwelcome application update, along with a sub-par quarterly earnings report, sent the stock spiraling down to $6 from its yearly high of $25. It had transitioned from an I.P.O. to a growth stock, to a deeply distressed asset. Guess what the financial pundits said when it dropped, "Sell, sell, sell."

Guess what I did; buy, buy, buy. And it paid off. Two years later, the stock was trading at $55.It gave me enough time to build a solid position and sell the initial invested principal as the stock regained traction. I felt comfortable letting the remainder ride and resting my originally invested cash for a new opportunity. In this instance, I suspected it would be around for at least five years, and probably much longer. For this reason, I kept the remainder as I foresee it having excellent future potential, and its "house money." Currently, it hovers around a gain of over 900% with zero principal invested.

Stocks going through growing pains, where the underlying business model and user base is solid, can be hidden gems. In today's markets, many investors are impatient. Temporary headwinds can make share prices sporadic. If the company is newer, it's not uncommon to require five to ten years to build a solid financial backing. If the user base is there and people love the product, the road to profitability is eventually found. Or they are acquired by an entity that can find it. Admittedly, it can be a riskier bet, that's not for the faint of heart. The proportion in your portfolio can help mitigate that risk by committing a smaller allocation percentage and having a variety of assets in your distressed bucket. Risk is further reduced by planning out previously discussed position scaling techniques.

Oil is an entire industry that is currently distressed. With the coronavirus limiting travel, oil utilization and demand is significantly suppressed. The valuation of individual securities in the industry often follows suit, resulting in shattering share prices.

Generally, I refrain from investing in the oil industry. It tends to be a laggard behind better opportunities. However, we sit in an interesting situation where it could be considered deeply distressed.

Although oil is a limited resource, and will eventually be depleted, at present day we rely on it heavily. Most experts suggest we have enough to last up to 50 more years at current consumption rates. That gives us a decade or two before panic emerges and to capitalize on volatility.

Right now, the consumption levels are historically low. When services heat up, I foresee them to do so with a vengeance over a time frame of one to two years. This presents a near term opportunity to swing in, and out of oil.

Notice that this strategy is different than most other mentioned securities. It is not a future industry or disruptor, but something that we depend on today. Alternative sources don't have the scale to power our world; Yet. Although oil is down, it is not out.

On the flip side, we have long term opportunities in the same industry. The alternate energy space. Luckily, we make our own rules and can benefit from both trends.

New/High Risk Sectors

Stocks with high volatility can leave you with sleepless nights and newly diagnosed GERD. They can also be the embroidered graphic on the tuchis of your newly purchased yacht after making you rich. Here, I'm going to discuss a new market with enormous potential, the marijuana sector.

Just over a year ago, the recreational use of pot was legalized in Canada. Companies quickly moved to the field to get in on the action. Despite enormous growth potential, there's a great degree of regulatory uncertainty. Agencies, such as the D.E.A., still haven't commented on the safety and effectiveness of marijuana's use.

As a pharmacist, I see great medicinal potential. From anxiety, depression, and pain control, there is a need for new product lines that are more approachable. The opioid epidemic exacerbates this need, as the safety profiles and addictiveness are a growing concern. Other available products have too many negative side effects or aren't adequate to control pain of greater severity.

For these reasons and others, I am an attentive buyer. But not until the hype died down. Knowing regulatory and supply chain issues would take time to master, I sat on the sidelines and watched many new to market I.P.O's hype themselves up two to five times their original price. Recently, they are making all-time lows, as slower than expected earnings and regulatory concerns were made public.

Looking to other countries can often be helpful in identifying trends. If Europe can turn black markets into government cash cows, why would the USA be any different? I think of the new marijuana sector like buying stock in alcohol pre-prohibition era. The industry has huge potential.

The trick with high-risk assets is buying slowly along our sliding scale. We want to exemplify our buy targets to error on the side of extreme caution and build robust positions as the assets drop. We'd also want to reduce the attribution to a smaller percentage of our total portfolio to further hinder risk. This will lower the impact of unforeseen headwinds, or incorrect speculation, on our overall portfolio value. Yet, we retain plenty of exposure to capitalize on long term gains, when and if the industry appreciates to the anticipated levels.

Chapter 11, Sorta...

Stocks going through bankruptcy carry the highest risk exposure imaginable, but they can heed large returns for shareholders if played appropriately. Most will steer clear of companies going through the process. In fact, many brokerages offer a warning notification when attempting to make a stock purchase into any companies that have filed. But this "common knowledge" sometimes leads to overt bargain pricing. You need to treat stocks in bankruptcy like a nature valley granola bar. If you dig in without a plan, the pieces will crumble to the floor.

A healthy turnaround can heed extreme gains for those courageous enough to take the plunge. It requires an unusual approach that would be frowned upon by the common man. But being uncommon here will give you the final laugh, all the way to the bank.

There are two types of bankruptcy. Chapter 11 and chapter 7. If there was such a thing as "good" bankruptcy, it would be chapter 11. This is often referred to as a bankruptcy protection phase, where the company tries to better position its finances to come out a stronger entity. Although well intentioned, it often fails. On the flip side, chapter 7 means a company is going completely out of business and operation stop.

The phase where we can score some serious coin is during chapter 11 bankruptcy proceedings. What initially occurs is the announcement. A company goes public about their plans to file chapter 11, and the share price shatters. Usually, on the order of 90% or more. Although this is detrimental to current shareholders, those on the sidelines can set up a large payday. Indeed, it is extremely risky, and should be approached with caution.

The time horizon here is usually short, ranging from 6 to 18 months. It greatly depends on the asset in question, but the stages go something like this.

- Chapter 11 announcement: Stock drops 90+ percent
- Company announces plan to reorganize its finances and operations
- Company proposes a settlement to creditors and bankruptcy judge
- Company secures financing to continue operations until the bankruptcy process is completed
- Plan is approved, and company pays creditors first, bondholders second, and shareholders last (usually nothing remains, and current shares are liquidated)

Buying into this nightmare comes with more warnings than a can of turpentine. But, if planned appropriately, you can secure gains with little risk exposure. Not only should you commit less than 2% of your total portfolio, but the extreme risks require a risk mitigated build strategy where we scale in like a turtle. Meaning, multiple buys with a large depreciation margin in sight for targets.

There are three stages where money can be made. The first is after the initial drop, the stock often rebounds in the hopes the downturn was overblown. Second, and of greater magnitude, when and if the company secures financing to continue operations, shares pop on the news. Third, the companies' efforts succeed, and they continue operations a stronger entity (rare).

There's a light at the end of the tunnel! But the door can close without warning. With different investment styles available in our artillery, swinging takes advantage of these temporary movements. Not the kind you need the wife's permission for (fat chance!). We will discuss later in greater detail.

A recent bankrupt company I traded was Hertz Global. A powerhouse in the car rental space, many labeled it too big to fail. With pandemic uncertainty luring, their operations are running at a dismal 20% of where it was a year ago. This made It a challenge to retain enough cash flow to keep the lights on. I scaled into a position upon news of the bankruptcy, and waited patiently for additional information to transpire. Averaging in at $0.82, I was able to swing out 5 times the principle weeks later on the rebound. I sold out 75% of my remaining exposure at the announcement of financing secured, when the stock soared 142% on the news. The remaining 25% was house money, left in the pot in hopes of a healthy turnaround. Eureka! My dream came true. Existing shareholders were paid out around $10 per share, and given issues of the new stock, a gain of over 1,000%. Time to find another stock to swing!

Stock Alternatives

I'm assuming most know about E.T.F.s and index funds. But I want to be complete in giving information for early investors.

You'll find abundance in financial texts that harp on just buying index funds or E.T.Fs. Rarely can you "beat the market," might as well "buy the market."

But after reading and understanding this book, you should be geared with tools needed to make you question, how can you not beat the market? Although these vehicles can offer a quick tool to gain diversified market exposure, utilized alone, they will kill your wealth potential. Let's briefly define each.

An index fund is a type of mutual fund that tracks a specific index, like Standard & Poor's 500 Index (S&P 500). It can also track companies separated by industry or size. They are not purchased on an exchange, but typically from your bank. Your investments will mirror the index whether it's up or down. They are a "hands off" approach to investing that require little maintenance and automate diversity. This translates to lower risk as well as lower potential returns.

Think of going to a bakery. They have hundreds of different selections of desserts. It can be hard to decide which craving you want to indulge in. But what if every dessert item was mashed together into one? That's an index fund in a nutshell. Luckily, they aren't edible. Index funds may have investment minimums and carry administrative and commission fees. Most are low, but don't assume so without research. Regardless, a fee is a fee and contributes to diminished returns. Index funds only trade once per day at market close. There is the constant rebalancing of the managed funds causing transactional fees and reducing tax efficiency.

An exchange traded fund (E.T.F.) is similar in that it tracks the performance of an index but can be traded just like stocks, throughout the day, on an exchange. They offer a high degree of diversity by compiling many stocks, without having to purchase each individually. Like an index fund, they often charge fees. The expense ratio is a percentage cost of ownership charged by the fund manager, used to cover operational expenses. These are usually lower than index funds. E.T.F.s are considered cheaper overall as there are often no commission fees. They can also be more tax efficient. Ensure to carefully review the prospectus to help identify investment quality and fee schedules.

Buying these types of funds can be a useful tool in diversifying your portfolio. But unless you like sub-par gains and paying fees, they aren't the best solo.

Mutual funds are similar but represent a more antiquated approach. Being actively managed comes high fees, that won't justify the damage to your wealth potential. Unless you are clueless and don't care to learn, steer clear.

People ask me why I don't like mutual funds. I could easily answer "fees" or "cookie cutter products," but most already know that. The majority of diversified mutual funds cannot allocate more than 5% of assets under management to a single investment. That sounds OK right? It is a good defensive strategy. But think about this. If a mutual fund allocated 2.5% of their fund into Tesla at a cost basis $30, and the share price rose to $60, EVERY subsequent gain thereafter would need to be sold (it's now trading around $700)

This is problematic for 2 reasons: 1) It destroys your earning potential, 2) Uncle Sam gets richer at your expense. Don't worry, your fees will still be safe and sound in your advisors (and the funds) pocket.

If a financial professional is pushing a fund on you, tell them you're late for a root canal. The best funds don't need a suit to convince you to buy them. Often, in exchange for hefty commissions and fees. The best funds sell themselves. If it feels like a sales pitch, it's a great indication that your returns will suffer. There is better way.

It never ceases to amaze me that people will hold mutual funds their entire life but wouldn't touch stocks with a 40-foot pole. That is like picking a Sara Lee turkey breast over grandma's thanksgiving turkey. Although they look similar, one is processed enough so you get extraordinarily little of what you think is inside. It's flavored to mimic the real thing, and costs about $5 more per pound. Despite this, the real bird takes skill and experience to cook. Try not to "Christmas Vacation" it.

Although E.T.F's may offer lower returns, they do have some utility. Financial institutions go to great lengths to create E.T.Fs. The prospectus of common E.T.F.s discloses what stocks or assets it's composed of, and in what amounts. You can also easily access this information through online brokerages like stash. Utilizing this information can be a good tool in discovering individual stock opportunities. If many E.T.F.s are holding the same stocks in high proportion, they are likely a quality investment to consider. But it is not a replacement for good judgment. Some funds contain large exposure to securities due to heavy share price appreciation. You still need to research whether it's plausible for that trend to continue. Review the funds' prospectus and potentially seek out high quality, individual companies that are held in heavy weight. Often, the top five to ten companies account for 50% or more of the fund. It would suit you better to purchase those individually and skip the fees, rather than buying the ETF.

Keeping them in a personal portfolio could be useful but holding for lengthy periods has limited risk. In conjunction with lower gains and reduced compounding potential due to fees, I generally reserve them for my I.R.A. account. This way I can truly set and forget my contributions and wake up at 65 knowing I'll have a healthy account balance to take disbursements from.

But I also want to build wealth I can enjoy early. That's where our personal portfolio comes into play.

The Day Trade Hype

Many have asked me if I am a trader or investor. Although I'd identify as ambidextrous here, the majority of my activity qualifies as long-term investing.

But which is better? The truth is you can earn money from both. But as they say, "the proof is in the pudding" The wealthiest 5 traders in the world have a COMBINED net worth of roughly $19 billion. The wealthiest 10 long term investors have an INDIVIDUAL net worth greater than $20 billion.

Wise girls emerge! Although there are many defined wealthy "traders" that are worthy, the ones with the highest net worth have obtained their wealth from various investment mechanisms. For the comparison above, I've focused on purism in trading versus long term investors.

Ever seen what someone at the gym that suddenly starts looking like the hulk? They've been hitting the weights for just a couple of months and surpass your lifelong efforts with ease and authority. Follow them closely enough and you'll eventually uncover the 23-gauge needles.

Taking steroids is like day trading. You may beef up your bank quickly at first, but only over time does your hair start clogging the drain. If you've ever seen a bodybuilder in their elder years, you have some insight into what most day trader's bank accounts looks like in retirement.

The lust of building wealth quickly is appealing, but the effects tend to wear off shortly after they kick in. Like gambling, the house eventually wins, and you keep coming back for more. If you are lucky enough to score big a few times, count on sharing it with your Uncle Sam to likes of 40%. Like going to the casino with a buddy, winning a grand, and paying him back the $400 he lost for being your wing man.

To be fair, skilled traders can make a "trade" of it. But that is their full-time job. Although there is potential to make a career of trading, it becomes exactly that. If you believe working for high salary is going to make you rich, head back to page one and start over. Although, I wouldn't mark it off as a high paying career. The average trader earns around $70,000 annually. Can they be wealthy too? It depends on what they do with the money. The type of wealth that is passed down via trusts though generations is rarely built or retained through these instruments alone. With long-term investing the margin of error is wider, as is the potential for wealth accumulation.[9]

If there is a place in your portfolio for day trading, keep the allotment to an amount that's unlikely to be negatively impactful, one to two percent. Or save that money for the tables, it's more fun.

---

[9] https://tradingsim.com/blog/day-trading-salary-how-much-can-you-really-make/

Swingers Welcome

Swing trading can be a useful tool in appropriate proportions of your portfolio. It is defined as a form of "active trading" that takes advantage of periodic swings in the stock price. They are usually held for a few days to a few months, capitalizing on short term price changes.

Like other securities we discussed, you can seek out low or high-risk opportunities. It involves researching where the stock will move next and more quickly buying and selling for a profit, then on to the next.

Due to substantial potential for rapid price fluctuations, I'd advise it to account for a small percentage of your portfolio; one to two percent. Again, this will depend largely on your individual risk tolerance. If it alludes to you, you may need to get physical with fundamental and technical analysis.

Nautilus Inc. is a company I've recently swung. During the coronavirus pandemic, gyms quickly became danger zones and temporarily closed their doors. This left many without their fitness fix cold turkey. Being on the fitness fanatic spectrum myself, I aimlessly searched for home fitness equipment. The Bowflex home gym and adjustable dumbbell systems popped to mind. Out of stock at major retailers like Walmart, Amazon, and eBay, I began to panic. Even the Bowflex website couldn't supply the demand. But saner ideas prevailed. I found a lightly used home gym unit on Facebook's marketplace for a steal. Whereas others were price gouging, this older couple had little use for it. In fact, they looked like they never used it. Kidding aside, it wasn't theirs. It was left behind by the previous owner of their newly purchased condo. A win-win. Fitness foes averted, my next thought, *Does Bowflex stock trade publicly?* Luckily, it did.

I discovered the parent company was a fitness titan composed of other brands like Nautilus, Octane, and Schwinn. Although an impressive assortment, the company struggled to find sustained revenue growth over the years. But things have changed, at least temporarily. It was clear the demand had ramped up enough to deplete the supply of most of their product offerings. I began deploying my swing trade reserve. Scooping up battered shares, the market had underpriced even further in the face of a pandemic, I secured my fair share of stock. I built a position along a sliding scale during the outbreak. As the pandemic pressed on, it was clear the trend would continue. Originally planning to sell the principle after quarterly earnings, I held strong. Legging into a robust position averaged around $2, I was sitting on gains of over 1000% after 6 months. Although the pandemic persists, I decided to sell out five times the original principle. Removing my principal risk and beyond, the trend may or may not continue. Either way, it's new capital to plant into my cash reserves, long term assets, or save for another brilliant swing.

Bond, Just Bonds

Bonds remind me of hand dryers in the bathroom of a highway rest station. They both have a similar magnitude of effectiveness in drying and making you rich. It usually takes long enough to give up and just wipe your hands on your new shirt. This book is an inappropriate medium to discuss bonds in detail. The intention is to get you on a wealthy path, not put you to sleep before the next page. There are plenty of resources available if you're in need of a restful night's sleep.

Bonds can be a great tool to mitigate risk. Generally, they don't make large movements, but pay a guaranteed coupon. They are less risky, and in turn, offer less reward. I'd consider them to be more of a wealth retainer than a builder.

Most books harp on bonds as a measure to build wealth, bury reserves to deploy under turmoil, or as a hedge against risk. After all, bonds and stocks are direct opposing forces, right? Wrong, both in magnitude in directions. Bonds barely move. Both of those mindsets are problematic. Historically, bond yields are pathetic compared to stocks. And they are not liquid enough to have flexibility in deploying at your leisure. But they do have utility in tax efficiency and wealth retention.

To me, a bond is like you lending someone money and collecting the interest. When you buy a house, you borrow money from the bank and guarantee to pay them a set amount of interest on the principal balance. Essentially, the bank owns the house and is letting you rent it from them in exchange for a fee. Buying a bond is like being the lender and getting guaranteed interest payments from the lendee until the loan is paid.

The only caveat is that you may have to hold them for a set period to guarantee receipt of the agreed upon interest. For my age, there is little reason to hold bonds in large proportion of my personal portfolio. That is the tool I use to build wealth efficiently. In fact, if you are young and not wealthy, I'd argue you don't need any bonds in your personal portfolio. Your money has time to weather whatever the market brings (you better have your rain boots ready).

Bonds do hold around 30% stake in my Roth I.R.A. account, mostly in the form of E.T.F.s and index funds. I don't plan on selling them till I'm old and gray, so the Roth is an excellent vehicle to park them in. I'd suggest to learn more about them once you've built measurable wealth. As you age, they have powerful utility in the retention stage. Or for fun, read any financial book on the market. They usually discuss bonds in great detail. The excitement is about equivalent to the returns you'll get from owning them.

Walking the Plank

So, when do you sell? This is the question I get asked most frequently. It reminds me of when my wife does my laundry. You have a relatively narrow window to take it out before it gets wrinkled or starts to smell like a wet dog. Although I like to strike while the iron is hot, not in this particular case.

Warren would say never and he's onto something. But we buy stocks to make money. Sometimes, we need to take some profits off the table. The simplest answer lies in one of his most famous quotes: "Be fearful when others are greedy, and greedy when others are fearful." Meaning, when experts emerge from the woodwork, it may be advisable to pull some profits. Or at the very least, build into your cash reserves fund.[10]

Like student loan refinancing, there isn't a one size fits all solution. Making the decision to sell is like learning to snowboard. It requires courage to make your decent down those first runs. I recall my first trails, being dropped at

---

[10]https://www.investopedia.com/articles/investing/012116/warren-buffett-be-fearful-when-others-are-greedy.asp

Cannon Mountain by my father in New Hampshire. He gave the board a go as well. Being an avid skier, frustration ensued quickly, throwing in the towel after the first run. After a full day on the slopes alone, I was left battered and bruised. Mostly in the gluteal region, but the passion to ride prevailed. After much patience and practice, it became second nature.

Although the answer isn't always clear, making decisions to sell swiftly is a learned art. It could be when one of your allotments grows too large; to the point where it takes up too much room in your portfolio and can make or break it. If that's the case, consider taking some off the table to redistribute or park as cash for the queen. It's easier, although still strategic, when you are sitting on massive gains.

Sometimes, stocks can rise quickly. A plausible approach may be to take the actual invested amount off the table and let the rest ride. If you originally invested $2,500, and it grew to $12,500, it's sensible to utilize the originally invested amount for cash reserves or an opportunity with better return potential. At that point, you can worry little about the remainder as its "house" money. The only risk is missing out on additional gains. Exercise solid judgment in determining if the remaining balance is an adequate amount to continue earning. If an opportunity is clear, you can choose to keep everything. If you auction off a portion, sell the allotments at a "loss," if available. I'll explain.

I recall doing this several times. An example that illustrates this is Zillow. In brainstorming and searching for stocks with enormous potential yet to be tapped, I came across the home "Zestimate" app. At the time, that was merely what it was. A way to find out what your friend's house is worth.

Although I'm a home ownership contrarian, I see both the buying and selling processes as antiquated and in need of disruption. Friends going through the process confirmed my perception. Zillow fits the bill with its massive user base that continues to grow. Over the years, it diversified a simple app into multiple facets of real estate. From an advertising titan, mortgage lender, agent finder, or home flipper, I've often described Zillow as the "Amazon" of homes, having a stranglehold on the real estate market.

I've owned the stock since 2015 through several growing pains. I bought a few shares during the stocks first hot cycle. At the time, the stock continued threatening to rise. Scared I'd miss gains, I bought a little more as part of a dollar cost averaging strategy. But eventually, it took a deep breath. My biggest buys were when a popular TV pundit was screaming sell. I don't watch financial reality tv shows, but am often lured into articles on Linked-in. I recall them screeching on their show, "What is Spencer doing?"

The CEO at the time was introducing the home flipping revenue stream. I disagreed with the host. Taking advantage of the turmoil, I was able to build a sizable position at a steal. It eventually grew to the largest position in my portfolio, accounting for over 25% of the personal portfolio allotment.

Although I love the stock and mission, I felt uncomfortable as my total portfolio started to solely mimic the performance of Zillow due to an overbearing position. For that reason, I took the opportunity to remove some principal from the table to the effect of unloading 25%. There were three advantages to selling here:

1. It still holds the largest position in my portfolio with a smaller amount of principal committed, still open to welcome massive returns
2. I was able to redistribute funds to my cash reserve bank, leaving mostly "house money" committed and begging the market to drop.
3. I sold older share allotments purchased at the highest price I paid for a small "loss," which is deductible from my income, despite a large total gain that continues growing.

The third point reiterates the importance of our buying strategy, or position scaling. A lot of the time, you won't necessarily be wrong, but may start building positions too early and pay a premium. This can be an advantage when the time comes to rebalance. For Zillow, my original buys were around $65. Most shares were purchased when opportunity rose, around $27. Since I decided to sell some when the stock rose back into the $60s, I opted to sell the early shares for a "loss." Due to a low average share price from a stringent position scaling strategy, the total gain percentage sat at nearly 100%. Selecting the higher share price allotment allowed me to deduct a total running gain as a "loss," once tax time emerged. Win-win.

We'll never be certain what temporary fluctuations will look like, but we can make an informed decision on the long-term trajectory of a stock. Looking back, I'm grateful Zillow dropped. Had it not, I wouldn't have been afforded the opportunity to construct a commanding position that greatly contributed to my current net worth. Today, it trades at nearly $200 per share. Along the ride upward, I continued removing principal commitments until getting a free ride, where risk has been removed. It currently sits as my largest position with negative principal risk. I even deducted a loss from my income! That is a good problem to have.

But, true love is when you can't live without someone. When you'd die if it fell apart. That was me and Zillow. Eventually, I bought it all back with reserves for a cheap price.

There's also a time and place to cut your general losses. If you realize the company in question has deteriorated and there's no hope in sight, you'll need to take some or all off the table. If we've mapped our portfolio responsibly, like the blueprints of an architect, no one position will spoil your gains. Learn from the experience. If 95% of your portfolio grows ten percent per year compounded, it will be more than okay. If one position accounting for five percent (or even an entire allocation bucket for that matter) deteriorates or goes to zero, it won't adversely interfere with the overall trajectory of your portfolio.

In attempt to standardize the selling approach, a good rule of thumb is to scale out of positions in a similar manner as you scaled in. It will greatly depend on the type of asset we are dealing with to determine what good looks like. Below, I have provided some general scale out suggestions for different security types to be used as a tool. I will typically follow this strategy, at least, until the principal is recovered. With very high-risk assets, I may continue using it even after the principal is recovered, as they are generally utilized for shorter time blocks to capitalize on gains. Think distressed and bankrupt. Again, do not let this replace good judgement. Keep in mind chapters "the players" and "great investors ask great questions" when determining the overall risk profile of a specific security.

Growth

- ❖ 25% gain: remove 5% of the entire position
- ❖ 50% gain: remove 10% of the remaining position
- ❖ 75% gain: remove 15% of the remaining position
- ❖ 100% gain: remove 20% of the remaining position
- ❖ 150% gain: remove 25% of the remaining position etc.

I.P.O's

- ❖ 25% gain: remove 10% of the entire position
- ❖ 50% gain: remove 15% of the remaining position
- ❖ 75% gain: remove 20% of the remaining position
- ❖ 100% gain: remove 25% of the remaining position
- ❖ 150% gain: remove 30% of the remaining position etc.

Big Caps

- ❖ 25% gain: remove 2.5% of the entire position
- ❖ 50% gain: remove 5% of the remaining position
- ❖ 75% gain: remove 7.5% of the remaining position

- ❖ 100% gain: remove 10% of the remaining position
- ❖ 150% gain: remove 12.5% of the remaining position etc.

Small caps

- ❖ 25% gain: remove 5% of the entire position
- ❖ 50% gain: remove 7.5% of the remaining position
- ❖ 75% gain: remove 10% of the remaining position
- ❖ 100% gain: removed 15% of the remaining position
- ❖ 150% gain: remove 17.5% of the remaining position etc.

New Markets

- ❖ 25% gain: remove 15% of the entire position
- ❖ 50% gain: remove 20% of the remaining position
- ❖ 75% gain: remove 25% of the remaining position
- ❖ 100% gain: remove 30% of the remaining position
- ❖ 150% gain: remove 35% of the remaining position etc.

Distressed

- ❖ 25% gain: remove 20% of the entire position
- ❖ 50% gain: remove 25% of the remaining position
- ❖ 75% gain: remove 30% of the remaining position
- ❖ 100% gain: remove 35% of the remaining position
- ❖ 150% gain: remove 40% of the remaining position etc.

Bankrupt

- ❖ 25% gain: remove 25% of the entire position
- ❖ 50% gain: remove 30% of the remaining position
- ❖ 75% gain: remove 35% of the remaining position
- ❖ 100% gain: remove 40% of the remaining position
- ❖ 150% gain: remove 45% of the remaining position etc.

To illustrate this strategy, let us say we build a position in the growth stock Zillow with $10,000 of principal, over a period of 6 months. After a year has passed, the position stands at a 25% gain, worth $12,500. At that point, we decide to remove $625 or 5%. We leave $11,875 remaining to continue earning. Another 3 months pass and we are sitting on a 50% total gain. We decide to remove and additional 10% of the remaining position. A few months further, we are sitting on a 75% total gain. We unload 15% of the remaining position. Onward 3 additional months, our position is sitting at a 100% total gain. We remove 20% of the remaining position. Continue to scale out in this manner until the principal is recovered, in this case $10,000, and the committed risk of for that position is eliminated. It doesn't always work out perfectly, and in many instances the stock will fluctuate back and forth. It is up to you to determine if drops in between are an opportunity to reallocate funds, or to continue letting it ride.

Scaling out of positions in the manner is beneficial in a few ways.

❖ You work towards recovering the principal to reduce risk exposure.

❖ You still leave ample funds committed to capitalize on further gains

❖ If the share price drops, your portfolio is impacted to a lower degree, and you retain cash reserves with the potential to amplify gains in that position or other opportunities that arise.

Hence, whether the share price rise or falls, you are setting yourself up for a win-win scenario. The riskier the asset in question, the quicker we scale out the principal and vice versa. Although these are suggestions, you create the scale based on your personal risk tolerance and the specific profile of the asset in question. The choice is yours. Once the principal is recovered, or even before, you do not need to scale anything out if you anticipate the upward trajectory to continue for the foreseeable future. If not, you can continue unloading or contributing as you see fit. This is simply illustrating ways you can reduce risk as positions transpire.

Platform Fever

Buying and selling stocks is a different game today. In the past, trading fees were a barrier to returns and the major determinant of selecting a platform. As of recently, most have moved to a model with no commission fees. This is a major win, as fees can significantly drag overall returns and reduce the power of compound interest, like dumping water on a fire. There are some newer players that haven't marketed their way to popularity yet.

Stash is my go-to for growth stocks, IPOs, or companies with hefty share prices. The major beauty is you can purchase partial shares. This allows you to easily distribute cash allotments into securities, without having to calculate amounts divisible by the share price. It also improves accessibility to companies with high share prices. Yes, you can buy pennies worth of Amazon or Tesla stock. Both are excellent growth stocks, but elsewhere, you'd need to fork out $1,000–$3,000 per share. What I really enjoy about stash is it slows down your emotional responses. Although not quite as sexy as live ticker prices, in the long run, the daily price fluctuations of securities matter very little. Unless your goal is to earn a few pennies. Actually, live tickers have devil-like intuition. Like a little voice on your shoulder, constantly telling you to do the opposite of what you should.

I also use Stash for my Roth I.R.A. account. It has a solid selection of E.T.F.s, bonds, and stocks that gives my retirement account the diversity and simplicity it needs to grow with confidence. Buying partial shares allows me to easily prorate allotments to selected securities without hassle. If I want to contribute $10 to each security weekly, the share price is a non-issue (even for ETFs, bonds, and Amazon!). I can "auto-stash" without digging out my calculator.

Caveats include limited access to individual securities (although rapidly improving) and limited buying blocks. At the time of this writing, Stash has two purchase windows; 10:30 a.m. and upon market close. This can in some ways be an advantage, but not having full access to all securities makes a second platform essential.

For everything else, it doesn't really matter. If trading commissions are free it depends on which is best suited for you. For me, *E*TRADE* does just fine. It offers many free tools and I'm accustomed to the user-friendly dashboard.

A few of the tools I'll utilize frequently:

- Analyst research reports.
- Fair value estimates and price targets.
- Earnings reports.
- Future earnings projections.
- Price to earnings ratios.
- Insider trades.
- Insider holding percentages vs. institutional holding percentages.

- Dividend yields.
- Financial articles.
- Operating/net margins.
- 52-week ranges.

Uncle Sam's Secrets

We'll try to be brief here. Plenty of books discuss the topic, but here's what you need to know. The goal is to keep as much of your nest egg to yourself. After all, you earned it! The biggest secret is wealthy individuals obtain most of their income from sources other than wages. Why? Wages are too expensive.

If you have $100,000 in wages, you'll take home around $62,000 after taxes. If you have $100,000 in long-term capital gains, you'll take home around $80,000 after taxes.

In addition, they strategically avoid paying taxes by using wealth as collateral to take out cheaper loans. Meaning, they don't sell investments in a way that would gather them a hefty tab from Uncle Sam. They balance losses and gains to orchestrate "low earnings," while their net worth soars.

Would you rather earn $100,000 of wages or have the collateral to take out a loan for $100,000 at 2.99% interest? The loan will cost you $2,999 dollars annually, whereas the wages will cost $38,000. Get the picture? Put another way, wealthy people have assets that grow at a faster pace than borrowing debt costs.

If you build a million-dollar portfolio, cashing out a $100,000 gain will cost you $20,000 in taxes. Or you can take out a $100,000 loan at 2.99% and pay the annual $2,999 in taxes, while allowing your assets to continue earning. If they average 10% annually, that $100,000 you borrowed will grow right back.

While the wealthy avoid high wages, the unwealthy fight for high wages. This is one of many reasons high wage earners need to keep earning. Another, they are rich, not wealthy. Although they can cover large monthly payments, they rarely have the assets or collateral to cover their lifestyle without working. When the earnings stop, so does the party.

We want to own most of our stocks for the long term, at least 12 months and 1 day. Meaning, if you purchase stock on April 18 2020, you need to wait until April 19 2021 to secure the long-term capital gain tax rates. This reduces your capital gains tax from around 40% to a range of zero to 20% based on your income and filing status. At this point, your flexibility in maneuvering positions improves. Sometimes, it makes sense to rebalance, realize gains or losses, or secure resources for better opportunities.

It's not always fun and games when a position goes sour. Like a bad relationship, we're tasked to determine if it's an opportunity, or if it's time to break things off. It's not you, it's me! If the reasons you bought the stock are no longer apparent, and deterioration is in sight, it may be time to take some or all off the table. Beware of confirmation bias. Often, investors scrounge for anything supportive of their decision to hold underperforming securities regardless of the outlook.

Luckily, you can deduct losses each year to reduce your taxable income, up to $3,000. Net losses exceeding this roll forward indefinitely! Although it's not quite a free lunch, you should take advantage of it yearly if applicable. You still want your overall portfolio to grow faster than the pace you take a yearly loss. If your portfolio grew 20%, from $100-120k, and you have some underperformers, you may want to scale out to some extent for better opportunities. Think about the most sensible place to deduct the $3,000 loss against your income. Keep in mind, the total realized gains and losses for your portfolios would need to show a negative value of $3,000. That means, if you realized some gains for the year, you'd have to balance them with losses to make it look like you "lost" $3,000. It won't always be sensible to do that, so use solid judgement here. If your portfolio grew significantly in value, and you can easily rebalance it to show a loss, do it. Or, if you have some positions with no hope in sight, unload. This will provide a boost to your tax return.

Our goal is to pick top notch securities and filter out duds. Sometimes, we are wrong or better opportunities arise. The strategies we put in place make that okay. Take a good look at your portfolio, at least annually, and be honest about mistakes. Reducing exposure to or selling off a position isn't the end. It's an opportunity for growth.

A second reason to bite the tax bullet is to take gains from active or swing trading. When you hit the right targets, it may be feasible to sell before the 12-month mark and "cut" your gains. Usually, this occurs inadvertently when a security rises faster than anticipated, to a level greater than expected. The stocks you trade actively (recommended not to exceed more than one to two percent if any) may have high volatility. It's possible any gains you made may be gone as quickly as they arrived.

Stein mart is one such example. My wife and I love visiting Florida. We'd move there if our families didn't enjoy being tortured by the cold and making snow angels. A store we always visit is Stein Mart. If you haven't been, it's essentially a high-class TJ Maxx or Ross's.

Monitoring hundreds of stocks, and being a customer, I fumbled across Stein Mart, ticker "Smart." Reviewing the chart, it had a history of violent swings and we were currently on the ground floor. I knew they had a big following in the southern states, and the semi-overblown retail apocalypse was in full swing. But I also knew it'd be unlikely for the company to go under any time soon. The stock was cheaper than dirt (a 40 lb. bag of scotts top-soil will run you $2.99), trading around $1/share. It had a significantly lower price to earnings ratio than its peers.

First time homebuyers always talk about how their current house isn't their "forever home." They'll build some "equity" and blow it on a bigger, shinier one when the monthly resources come along. This is how I felt about Stein Mart. But I also smelled value. It had been around for a while, carried excellent name-brand products at great values, a sizable repeat customer base, and several hundred stores still operating. If things were to end, it would take some time to wean out under performers and restructure before ultimately closing shop. The business was under distress, but the stock was trading like the company filed for chapter 11.

I also saw the company as a likely "buyout" story for players like TJX, rather than a bankruptcy. I dipped my toes in slowly, and patiently waited for further drops to take advantage of. My lowest and largest purchase along my position scaled targets was at $0.64. I had a sizable number of shares at a cheap price, and the position took up under two percent of my portfolio. If the waves got choppy, the remaining allocations in my portfolio wouldn't feel the wake. But they didn't get choppy, and to this day, it is one of the larger swing trade gain percentages I've realized.

Due to a mixture of factors, namely a positive earnings report, yearly outlook, and cost cutting initiatives, the stock skyrocketed. Although I felt like a genius when the stock was trading at $3.65, I also knew things could revert as quickly as they arrived. Check out the chart for yourself.

Stein Mart had a high-risk profile and had become a larger percentage of my portfolio than I was comfortable with. After the share appreciation, almost 500%, it accounted for around 10% of my portfolio. If the meteoric rise was a tried-and-true big cap like Disney, I'd sleep better at night holding it long term. I made the judgment to deplete the entire position prior to the 12-month mark and bit the bullet on paying the 40% capital gains tax. 12 months later, the stock was trading back at $0.60. And for the record, I am still a shopper, and it didn't go bankrupt. The company was taken private by Kingwood capital at $0.90 per share.

These are the instances I can condone selling "early:"

1. Positions that grow to overbearing levels that could have a significant negative impact on your overall

portfolio, and retain large commitments of principal.

2. Swing trades.
3. Incorrect assessments.
4. Inadvertent home runs

Everything else, you want to build positions slowly and plan on a happy marriage. If you're lucky, the ride to the top will be bumpy. Pay particular attention the buying strategies discussed previously to capitalize on turmoil.

In contrast to Stein Mart, TESLA was a stock I stalked for a while. It was notoriously "overvalued" in the investment world. Admittedly, I was quite the secret admirer. Short sellers loved to batter the stock. They'd post article after article theorizing why the stock would crash (On a side note, this is often a good sign. In the investment world, they are called "detractors"). But electric vehicles are here to stay, and the industry is growing quickly. The car industry in general is shifting from gas combustion vehicles to electric vehicles (hence why Tesla is not producing gas engines). This potential to capitalize on market share is huge. With most traditional automakers behind the 8-ball, Tesla has a big lead and durable competitive advantage. TESLA was the first to market and has a product with technology that others will take years to catch up to. They are considered a disruptor to multiple existing industries (two key ingredients often seen in massive growth animals).

Most articles written today focus on today's earnings, rather than future growth potential. They look at the "sticker price" and say "it's a bubble, it's going to crash!" or "that is expensive!" That is ordinary thinking that heeds ordinary returns. Rhetoric often indicative of "missing the boat" that spreads imagined danger, preventing bystanders from building wealth.

One of the main reasons' stocks rise is investors realizing the company's potential tomorrow. It follows that many of your biggest gains will come from companies that are "overpriced" today, and they will be even more "overpriced" in the future. "Underpriced" companies are usually so for a reason. As previously discussed, they have a different utility. Most people are stuck in the "buy low, sell high" mindset. That certainly holds true. But if you want to earn more, change the music. You can also buy high and sell higher.

I had the opportunity to own a TESLA and the experience was remarkable. Going from driving the spaceship-like machine to my wife's new gas guzzler, felt like powering up an old flip phone. I also saw the company as more than a car producer. They are the closest answer we have to clean, sustainable energy in the future. They are disruptors in the power utility business.

Thinking of the needed time it would take other manufacturers to catch up; they could potentially be a supplier of batteries to other automakers. Having the charging infrastructure, better range, and more power, why not? Their batteries could also expand to locomotives like planes, trains, or even power your home. They already do some work with solar panels. The potential to power anything is imminent.

I came across an opportunity where a storm of bad information was grinding the stock down to the bone. It fell about 20% when I started testing the waters. It continued to drop past the 50% mark, and a light flickered in my brain. I needed more. Although the water was cold, I believed in the mission and visionary leadership enough to muster the strength to submerge under. I was able to build my full position and beyond into my growth bucket. Like the 1980 USA Olympic hockey team, one of the biggest upsets in sports history, beating USSR for the gold 4-3. I was quickly sitting on more than 2000% gains. Every $100 purchased against the rhetoric is worth over $2,500 today and rising. Eat that, shorts! Financial "experts" will still bash it. I say, talk to me when they power your fake Rolex.

In contrast to physical retailer Stein Mart (refresher: we swung a distressed asset to take advantage of short-term movement), where online shopping is the future, TESLA is the future in its industry. For that reason, I am comfortable holding onto most of the position for the long term. I don't foresee many scenarios I'd be comfortable selling out completely, but as previously discussed, I did follow scale-out procedures to recover the principal and then some. When people talk to me about risk and TESLA, I have the luxury of saying, what risk? Here, it's not worth taking any short-term gains and sharing with Uncle Sam.

Specifically, I was able to sell out five times the original principal invested. I removed my principal risk, and in fact negated it, while leaving enough present to continue the summit. Will the road continue to be rocky? I hope so, but the end game has growth and market share written in permanent ink. Every opportunity has a shelf life. If you find a disruptor leading a new industry, and there is little doubt of success, capitalize. Especially during turmoil when the common rhetoric is not to.

You also want to take advantage of vehicles such as your 401K and I.R.A. accounts. If you are single, or married and have a combined low income, the traditional Roth is the best path. Eligible parties can deduct up to $6,500 worth of contributions as of this writing.

If you have a high individual or family salary, the Roth I.R.A. is the way to go. Although there is no standard deduction, this money is pre-taxed. This means any withdrawals after 65 will be tax-free, unlike the 401k.

In comparison, the 401k allows you to contribute gross income and grows tax-free. Your contributions are deductible, allowing a healthier annual tax return. As of this writing, you can deduct up to $19,500. Keep in mind that number does *not* include the company match. You can deduct the yearly amount of your own contributions. The match is a bonus.

At minimum, you should contribute to the max company match, but I'd recommend taking advantage of the $19,500. Especially during periods that the market is high and due for correction. This allows you to reduce your income when things are good. As history suggests, markets will likely tread higher in the future, but the near term should present plenty of opportunities. When turmoil comes, you can reduce your 401k contributions back down to the company match. This allows you to have more cash available to deploy to higher returning investment vehicles. Although the 401k is a safer haven, its likely you will earn more in stocks coming out of corrections. Most of us want to enjoy wealth prior to getting checked into a nursing home. That's the job of your personal portfolio. 401ks and I.R.A.s ensure whatever happens with your personal portfolio, you are set up for success in retirement. I'd strongly suggest utilizing both in conjunction.

Currently, we are enjoying tax levels that are the lowest in history, although they seem high to us. We don't know what the future will bring from a taxation point, but if taxes go up, your 401k distributions will suffer in retirement. The I.R.A. will be your crutch. Again, contributions have already been taxed and are withdrawn tax-free.

There are also some bonds that can reduce your tax drag. Municipal bond interest offers a hall pass from federal income taxes. In addition, you may get out of paying state income taxes on interest if they were issued in the state you work.

US treasury bonds, backed by the government, also offer interest-free of state income taxes. As a heads up, you'll want to purchase these types of bonds outside of your I.R.A. accounts to capitalize fully on tax-free advantages.

Credit Crunch

I'd rarely recommended taking out money on margin from a broker. That is welcoming amplified losses. And, you have to pay the money back with interest, plus be prepared for any margin calls if the market tanks. But there is a way you can get interest free money quickly. No, not to buy more stuff and stash it in the garage, but to build your portfolio.

Depending on your credit score, some banks will beg you to take an interest free line of credit. Their goal is to get you into financial checkmate, when the interest free promotional period stops rolling, they hit you with more than 20% percent interest on your remaining balance. The trick is to utilize new offers to transfer balances before the vigor starts running. Many times, you can find new offers that have no balance transfer fee, or as little as three percent. Check out nerdwallet.com for best offers. This sounds like a terrible idea, but it's much less than the eight percent margin a broker will charge you, or the 25% you'll get charged when the credit card vigor kicks in.

If utilized appropriately, you can trade market gains, (again the average is ten percent, but I hope you now understand you can do better) for zero to three percent interest and collect the spread between charged interest and your investment gain percentage. It's not for everyone, but if managed appropriately, utilizing credit can contribute to building wealth faster. Finding cards that give incentive cash back can be a double whammy.

So, do I buy the stocks with my credit card? No, I utilize the card for small expenses such as groceries, gas, utilities, etc. The extra money from your income is then used to purchase stocks, less the monthly credit card payment. If you have two to three different lines of credit, they will generally beg you to get money back to that account with interest free checks. If you rotate back and forth during the interest free cycles, it frees up a little more cash to invest in opportunities that arise.

I recently received an email from my bank offering a credit summary for the year. They thanked me for being a customer. But, I should have been the one thanking them. On this card, I had transferred a balance of $15,000 in exchange for a 3% balance transfer fee, or $450. We traded the balance for 12 months of interest free payments. Sounds hefty, right? It depends. There are three types of credit customers: 1) those who get in over their heads, 2) those who try to build credit scores and become "debt free," 3) those who leverage credit in exchange for income. I chose #3. That $15,000 balance, of which I paid the minimum payment, was leveraged to obtain a 211% gain creating a balance of $46,650 over the 12-month deferral period. Meaning, instead of paying off the balance with my cash, I invested it strategically into higher appreciating assets. That $450 fee doesn't look so bad anymore. The deferred balance was leveraged to earn an additional $31,650 in annual income.

But this should never exceed five to ten percent of your portfolio, depending on risk tolerance. If the value of your portfolio is $250,000, you should never carry a combined credit balance of more than $25,000. Less is preferable. You want to be able to quickly knock out that debt if the need arises. Having a ten to twenty times greater portfolio balance gives you a large cushion to do so quickly, should the need arise, negating any risk.

Am I Rich Yet?

Many investors feverishly monitor their portfolios for the wrong reasons. Am I rich yet? Did I lose or gain money today?

Building an elite portfolio relies on some degree of turmoil. Watching daily stock fluctuations for the sake of monitoring success is like checking the mirror on the first day of a new diet. It isn't impactful in the long run. Unless you're looking to make a few pennies. The daily gains and losses are miniscule in the grand scheme. In fact, many days, I don't even look at my portfolio.

I get frustrated when stocks rise, and happy when they fall. Originally, I wished I had a lot of money at once to invest. Luckily, I never came across Aladdin's magical lamp. As I gained experience, I realized having a stable income (or revenue stream) to invest continuously over time is much more valuable. Time will make the daily fluctuations appear like a grain of sand on endless ocean shores. It is your friend. Luckily, in smaller blocks, the fluctuations seem measurable, so you have sizable windows to build your positions, taking advantage of temporary downfalls along the way.

The only variable I use to monitor my portfolio is the "total gain percentage." I want this to be in the red when I'm building new positions, and sometimes even with old friends. Welcoming, and even craving volatility, I want to be "wrong" initially so I can construct a robust position before true value emerges. Or get the opportunity to do so for a good company that is facing temporary headwinds. For, building an elite portfolio depends on it.

Nothing but Net

The key indicator to determine wealth isn't measured by the size of your monthly payments, but your total net worth. Adding up all your assets and subtracting your liabilities gives you a snapshot at a given time. I recommend calculating it quarterly to confirm you're on the right track.

Check out the example calculation below. You can choose to include your vehicles as you see fit. Some may really be an asset. There exists a market for rare collectables, as there does for stocks. For mine, I consider the "equity" I've built as an asset, as it will translate to cash. In the example below, If Pete sells his truck over the next three months, he should comfortably retain $10,000 more than he owes. The same is true for your home. If you own a $400,000 home, but owe the bank $375,000, you'd include the equity minus transactional costs to sell (and other expenses) as an asset.

Pete's Assets
Vehicle equity if sold today: $10,000.
Savings: $25,200.
401K: $200,000.
Roth I.R.A.: $15,750.

E*TRADE portfolio: $193,500.

Stash portfolio: $ 150,300.

Company stock purchasing plan: $25,000.

Home equity: $15,000

Total assets: $634,750.

Pete's Liabilities

Student loan: $90,000.

Credit card debt: $20,000.

Total liabilities: $110,000.

Net worth: $524,750.

In general, Net worth should improve quarterly as you simultaneously invest and attack debts. It won't always be the case, as changing market conditions and even corrections are inevitable. But with the strategies discussed in this book, net worth reductions due to turmoil should be a temporary opportunity to build wealth beyond what was previously possible. You should also utilize major indices like the Dow Jones and S&P 500 to compare your returns. If the indexes are consistently outperforming your portfolio, it may be time to reassess your holdings and strategies. Try plan B. Sometimes, you need to get a little further in the alphabet to discover a successful formula. The hope is, I have exposed the path for you.

Measure Twice, Cut Once

It's time to take action! When people understand what they need to do to be successful and the attributes needed to build wealth, they can achieve financial freedom. I wrote this book with you in mind. The greatest fulfillment comes through the empowerment of helping others. My hope is it will help the next generation understand investing, and gain the tools needed to achieve desired financial outcomes. Pass the knowledge along and make other people better. Remove self-imposed limitations. Make your dreams a priority.

Investing is a lifestyle; it's not a one-time thing. You get exactly what you put in (plus appreciation, dividends, and compound interest). A lot of time will be spent planning, improving, and recognizing opportunities, with a pinch of discipline, balance, and emotional intellect. Like a tailor, you'll need to measure twice and cut once. The process isn't always easy. It takes willpower. There will be moments of struggle and uncertainty.

This book is not about the habits of the poor or middle class. It's not about being "comfortable," lust, or desires. It's about the habits of the wealthy. It isn't the standard path, but the exception.

Investing successfully isn't a rubber stamp to wealth the uniformed can achieve by any stretch of the imagination. It can be a high wire act. Many without just knowledge have "lost their shirt." Make a courageous plan and don't look back. Don't deny yourself the life you deserve, fearing what others will think or because it's too risky. Often, we know what doesn't work, yet give in to the empty desires of ourselves or others. Wealth is available to you and time is of the essence.

Undoubtedly, building wealth takes persistence and patience. It's a roller coaster ride comprised of all-time highs and painful lows. It can present chaos and confusion. Giantess won't be achieved in comfort zones. If you keep pushing through the finish line utilizing learned strategies, triumph will emerge. Seek out the path of lowest risk in exchange for the highest rewards. The best investors are risk mitigators.

Fall in love with the journey and set financial goals that make you want to jump out of bed. The tools provided will help you navigate challenges with a high degree of confidence. If you consistently "pay yourself first" and invest strategically, you'll be sitting well in good time.

I hope you feel like you got more than your money's worth from this book and it helped drive the mission of financial freedom into your heart. If you don't decide what your worth, someone else will. The clock starts now. Only you can choose what your future holds. Now "be quiet" and go get wealthy!

End